For My Grandchildren
Isabelle, Emma, Madison, Chloe, Bode, Lucy, and Wren

STEWARDSHIP

Every part of this earth is sacred.
Every single pine needle, every shore,
every mist in the dark woods, every
clearing, every humming insect is
holy in the memory and experience of
our race. You are part of the earth
and the earth is part of you.

You did not weave the web of life, you
are merely a strand in it. Whatever
you do to the web, you do to yourself.
You may think you own the land. You
do not. It is God's. The earth is
precious to him and to harm the earth
is to heap contempt on its Creator.

Love the land as those who have gone
before you have loved it. Hold in your
mind the memory of the land as it
is when you take it.

And with all your strength, with all your
mind, with all your heart, preserve
it for your children and love it...
as God loves us all.

—Chief Seattle, 1854

TABLE OF CONTENTS

ACKNOWLEDGEMENTS

Thanks to all the people who bought my first book "Some Just Get Away..."and encouraged me to write this second book. I hope everyone will enjoy, "Give Me A Break!"

Thanks to all my family and friends that helped and encouraged me with "Give Me A Break!"

I would like to thank the people who helped me by proof-reading this book-my daughter Heidi, my friend Ross and Ione Bryant, who taught me the difference between thawed and unthawed!

Thank you Chris Hedin for illustrating my book. I didn't think I would ever find another artist like the late Cliff Letty, but you met all my expectations. I know Cliff would be proud of your work also. Thanks for the wonderful job, Chris!

FOREWORD

I first met Curt Rossow when he took the position of Game Warden at the Willow River, Minnesota station in 1975. I didn't get to work with Curt until the fall of 1975. After working with him, I was impressed with his sincere dedication to the resources and the people of Minnesota.

Curt was willing to work extra hours to get the job done. He was always pleasant to be with and work with. He treated violators with respect and politeness.

Curt taught young people to respect our laws and wildlife. He gained the respect of city, county and state officials as well as the citizens of his area. The citizens thought enough of him to elect him as a county commissioner after his retirement as a game warden/conservation officer.

Curt, I was proud to work with you those many years. I appreciate that you always remembered me with visits after my retirement.

I wish you and Martha the best in your retirement years.

The following book is a factual, exciting and often amusing account of Curt's adventures.

—Jim Bryant
Fellow retired Game Warden/Conservation Officer
Isle, Minnesota

Me repairing a boat ramp on Island Lake.

FISHING SHORTS

One winter day, I was on Sand Lake checking fishermen. I often wore a jacket liner over my uniform. I did this so potential violators would not identify me before I had a chance to get close to them to observe any violations that might be taking place. I stopped at a dark house that seemed to be occupied. I knocked on the door and a male voice said, "Come in." I entered and observed an older gentlemen staring down a large hole in the ice while watching his artificial decoy. He was spearing northern pike. His spear was propped up over the hole in the ready position. I asked him if he'd had any luck. He said that he hadn't. I enjoyed looking down a spear hole, it was like looking into an aquarium. I was intending to check his licenses, but first I wanted to observe his sport. We engaged in some small talk. All of a sudden the fisherman said, "I haven't speared a walleye in a number of years." My ears perked up, because it was illegal to spear walleyes! Then my fisherman friend said, "By the way, who are you?" I said, "I'm the game warden." Boy, did he get a surprised look on his face. I checked his licenses and all was in order. I found out that he made his own spearing decoys. Max became a good friend. He taught me how he made his decoys.

One of our jobs as a Conservation Officer was to check boaters for proper equipment. One important item every boater needed was enough life jackets for each person in the watercraft. Often, I would find someone without a life jacket. Some would say that they were good, great or life saving swimmers. I told them that I couldn't be responsible for their safety, nor did I have the time to have them jump in the lake with their clothes on and swim to shore and back.

One incident that didn't make me happy was when I checked a father with two little children on Sturgeon Lake one day. He didn't have one life saving device on board! I told him that I was going to give him a ticket. He told me that he was a trained life saving swimmer. I asked him which child he would save if one fell over one side of the boat and the other fell over the other side at the same time. He thought for a second and said, "That's a good question." He accepted the ticket and left the lake to get life jackets. The fine was $20.00 in 1976.

I would often take time off and go visit my good friend and fellow Game Warden Bob Kangas. I first met Bob when he was stationed in Hinckley, Minnesota. He was my neighboring officer. We worked together and became friends. Bob moved up north to the Schroeder Station.

Although we would take a little time off to do some fishing, we were always alert for violations. One day I was riding with Bob on the "grade." We passed a lake right along side of the grade. There was a cut in the bank down to the lake. I observed two people, one of them fishing. Bob could not see them from the drivers side. I told Bob that there was a guy fishing without a license. He asked me how I knew that. I told him the guy was reeling a spinning rod and reel outfit upside down and backwards! He obviously didn't know much about how to fish. Bob agreed that I was probably right. We went down the road and turned around. Bob checked the individual for a fishing license-he didn't have one. Bob issued him a summons. Bob was upset when we finished and left the violator. Bob was upset because he was a local person who knew Bob was the Game Warden and still had the audacity to break a fish and game law!

Every conservation officer has a few good repeat customers. I had one on Big Pine Lake. In early January 1980, I caught the individual fishing without a license. I issued him a ticket and he paid a fine of $25.00.

In August 1983, I observed an unattended fishing line off a dock on Big Pine Lake. Upon checking the ownership of the dock and line, I discovered it was the same individual that I had ticketed three years earlier. He was given another ticket and paid a $27.50 fine.

In May of 1992, while checking fishermen on Big Pine Lake, I observed an individual fishing with two lines. You guessed it, the same guy again! His fine this time was $60.00. I never caught him doing anything wrong after that. He either gave up fishing or decided the fines were getting to high to violate again.

2

BORDER WARDEN

Being stationed on the border with Wisconsin, we Minnesota Conservation Officers were deputized Wisconsin Deputy Game Wardens. This is so a violator couldn't just run across the border to get away from us. Also, Wisconsin and Minnesota officers could assist one another.

Being in a border station we met and knew sportsmen from the other state.

One early summer, my neighboring officer Pete Jensen from Hinckley received a call that an individual from just across the border in Wisconsin had bought a fawn deer from a Minnesota resident who had captured it from the wild. The individual who bought the buck fawn was going to use it on his game farm. Pete and I both knew the individual and had a good relationship with him. Pete asked me to help. Pete contacted the warden from Wisconsin.

We met the Wisconsin warden just across the border very early on the 4th of July. The Wisconsin warden said that he had a number of law enforcement officers ready to block off the roads, in case the individual tried to flee. Pete and I both said that would not be necessary. We both knew the individual and thought that when confronted with the information he would come clean.

The three of us arrived at the individual's residence. We knocked on the door. The individual stuck his head out of an upstairs window. He immediately recognized Pete and I. He said, "Hi Curt, hi Pete, come on in." He welcomed us into his breakfast nook. He offered us breakfast. We said thanks, but no thanks. He offered us something to drink. Pete had coffee. I had a soda pop. The young Wisconsin warden didn't want anything. Pete, myself and the individual proceeded to talk about fishing and hunting and more or less just had a friendly conversation. (Some people called us conversation officers!) This went on for some time. The young Wisconsin officer finally couldn't take it any more. He said, "This is bull....!" I then calmly told the individual, "I suppose you know why we are here." The individual said, "I suppose it's about that fawn I bought in Minnesota." He knew that we hadn't just shown up to shoot the breeze. He told us the whole story. He showed us where the fawn was and we seized it. Pete gave him a receipt for the fawn and a ticket. I'll bet the young Wisconsin warden is still shaking his head. He thought it was going to be a lot harder than it was! Pete followed up on the individual who had taken the fawn from the wild.

Fawn deer.

3

BEARS I HAVE KNOWN

At one time bears were unprotected. They could be shot anytime of the year for any reason. A few bear were shot every year during deer hunting season. Some were shot because they were doing damage to property or agricultural field crops. Some were shot out of fear that they might hurt or kill humans. Some were shot for food. Because of this uncontrolled killing, bears appeared to be rather scarce. It was rare, when I first got to Willow River, when someone told me that they had seen a bear. The Department of Natural Resources decided to control the bear harvest. They did this by making the bear a big game animal, setting a season for their taking and limiting the number of people that could hunt them each year. Other rules, such as methods of taking and no cubs were instituted. This seemed to greatly increase the bear population! With the increased population and protection, the complaints of nuisance bear increased. Conservation officers were there to receive and adjudicate the complaints. We did that in a number of ways. We tried to educate people on how to live with the bears. We would live trap and move bears. We would get bear hunters and landowners together and as a last resort kill the problem bears ourselves or issue permits to individuals to take the problem bear(s).

On a late December day, I received a call about a bear hanging around in a yard east of Kerrick, Minnesota. The bear had been there for four days. When I got there the bear was up a large elm tree right next to the house. When asked what the bear was doing, (I asked the homeowner, not the bear!) I was told it just kept walking around the house and looking in the windows. I could see a potential problem. The homeowners had named the bear (Honey Bear) and didn't want to see it hurt! I told them it looked like a two year old and probably a male. Isn't it the young males that are always getting into trouble?! I set a live trap next to the house to catch the bear. Honey Bear ignored the trap. It just hung around the house sitting on the porch behaving its self. The homeowners were getting a little nervous, and called me to come and tranquilize Honey Bear. On the way out to their place, I was going over in my mind how I was going to break the news to the homeowners that we didn't have the ability or desire to tranquilize bear. I lucked out and the bear had left, scared by a cattle truck coming into the yard after a thirteen day stay! I read about the bear, homeowner and my exploits that Thursday in the editorial column in the local newspaper!

Honey Bear's adventures (and mine) were not over yet. A bear showed up at Dutch Jones' residence down the road from Honey Bear's previous escapades. It sure sounded like the same bear. The bear hung around on her deck, knocked down her bird feeders and bird houses, ate the dog food and uncovered her flowers! Dutch was very patient until the bear (whose name had been changed to Sugar Bear!) chased her back into the house one day. Quoting Dave Heiller, the editor of the *Askov American*, (Yes, we made his column again!) "Sugar Bear got off on the wrong foot by chasing Dutch around, shooing her back into the house as she went to the car one day. There aren't many men that could shoo Dutch Jones into her house, let alone a bear on the verge of puberty." Dutch called me. I went out to her place that night. Enough was enough. I brought my 30-06. The bear came out of the dog house as I pulled into the yard. It went up the willow tree right behind the dog house. I went inside and told Dutch what I had to do. A neighbor was there with his deer rifle and offered to back me up. I told him to stay in the house. I didn't want any would be hero behind me in the dark with a loaded gun! Sugar Bear (Honey Bear) was dispatched humanely. A post script: We lost Dave in 2007, He will be missed and was always fair to me in his editorials.

I received a call one fall from a gentleman east of Bruno, Minnesota. He was a trapper and had caught a bear cub in one of his coyote sets. He wanted help releasing the cub. I grabbed my catch pole and took off for his place. The cub was caught in a field set. That was good, because the cub was making an awful fuss and we needed to have room to observe if the mother bear was going to come to her cub's rescue. The cub's foot did not appear injured. I put the catch pole over the cubs neck and stretched the cub out against the trap anchor. The older gentlemen released the trap from the cub's back foot. The cub was out of the catch pole and running by me before I even had time to release the catch pole!

One January, my neighboring officer, John, called me to give him a hand. It seems some loggers in his area had moved a brush pile and uncovered a bear den. The sow bear had run off and there were cubs left in the den. We arrived at the den. I carried my 30-06 in case there were problems with the mother bear. John crawled into the den and came out with three cubs. The cubs were about 2-3 pounds each. Their eyes were still closed and they were very cold and stiff. We weren't sure if they were still alive or would make it. We put them on the dash of our squad and turned the defrost on high. We noticed some movement. We cupped our hands over their mouths and blew our hot breath into the cubs, sort of mouth to mouth! The cubs were alive! John took them home and placed them on his oven door to warm them. He fed them some milk replacer. The next day he asked for my help again. We were going to try and get the cubs back with their mother. I again held the gun. John had purchased a couple of chemical heating pads to keep the small cubs warm until their mother returned to them. John placed them back in the den on the heating pads. We then left. John monitored the situation. The sow returned, removed and relocated each cub! He could tell by the tracks in the snow. He did not follow them to their new den site. He figured that they had suffered enough trauma.

Black bear in live trap.

4

SAVING FACE

As a conservation officer, I never tried to belittle a violator in front of his or her peers. I often would hear stories how one of my arrests went, and wondered if I had even been there!

One day checking fishermen on Sand Lake, I came across a boat with three gentlemen fishing. The fisherman in the back was using two lines. I checked the front two for licenses, which they had and they just kept busy fishing. I asked the violator for his license. He gave it to me. I didn't have to say a word, I just wrote out the ticket and told him to sign it, which he did. I gave him his copy, told them to have a nice day and left. I don't think his two buddies even knew he had gotten a ticket. I wonder if he ever told them?

One night while checking smelters on Grindstone Lake, I observed an individual in the Grindstone River actively dipping for smelt with a dip net. I called him to shore and asked to see his fishing license. He didn't have one. I issued him a ticket for fishing without a license. He paid his fine. The individual was a prominent businessman in a local community. The story got back to me that he was just handing the net from the trunk of his car to someone else when he was given the ticket! I did correct this slight misinterpretation of facts whenever I was asked about this arrest.

Winter fishermen would look out the door of their fish house whenever they heard someone approaching, especially if they were doing something wrong! Jim Bryant, the retired Game Warden from Isle, Minnesota, called these individuals "Johnny jump ups."

I was approaching a fish house on Sturgeon Lake on my snowmobile, the individual popped out of his house and looked my way. The individual rushed back into the house. I hurried to the house suspecting the individual had too many lines down and was going to try to clean them up. By this I mean they would try to pull up the extra lines or cut them. I got to the house and inside before the fisherman could accomplish the task. The fisherman had a bloody hand. I asked him what had happened and he said that he tried to break the monofilament line with his hands because he didn't have a knife. He had broken one line, but above the bobber! He was given a ticket for fishing with an extra line.

The story I heard later, was that I had missed another line he had down in the corner. That didn't happen. He was just trying to save a little face with his buddies by saying that he had beaten me on a violation.

5

COMEDY OF ERRORS

Deer shining use to be a popular past time. People would go out at night usually in the fall of the year and shine lights on fields to locate deer feeding that they then could shoot. During the depression years families needed this extra meat to survive. As the generations passed, less and less people needed the meat, but still did it. Shining declined during my tenure as a conservation officer. Probably not because of me, but the fines, lose of vehicles and equipment made it less worthwhile. Also, now with all the bonus deer an individual may take-who wants another deer?

In the fall of the year we would have shining crews. A crew was around four squads with two officers each spaced in likely locations covering 15-20 miles. The local officer would decide on these locations and then get a map to our "eye in the sky." Our "eye in the sky" was a conservation officer pilot. They would circle the area and spot vehicles shining fields and direct the nearest squad(s) to the location and the vehicle to stop. Sometimes the weather would prevent the pilots from flying, if plans had been made the work crew went on as scheduled. When Ray Sanbeck was my supervisor we were a well oiled machine!

Ray went on to bigger and better (?) things in the St. Paul office. How could things get any better then field work? This meant we had to break in a new supervisor!

That fall I organized a shining work crew. I had five squads and locations set up. Bob would drive one squad with our new supervisor. Bob was new to the area, so I took my supervisor during the day and showed him the spot to sit that night. I told him not to drive unto the hayfield because the farmer had spiked the field. Spiking the field meant the farmer had placed a board with spikes sticking out of it across the access road to the field. In theory the bad guys would drive across these and get flat tires.

The three other squads had two conservation officers a piece. I would drive the fifth squad and my passenger was a good friend and state employee from the tree nursery. The weather turned, so our eye in the sky was unable to work that night. I made the mistake of bragging to my passenger what a well oiled machine he was going to witness! First radio silence is a must-the bad guys sometimes monitored our radio.

The first indication things were falling apart was when one squad showed up late, and after being in position for only a short time, got on the radio and said that they had finished their lunch and were going home! I had placed them in a good location and thought they might get some action.

Next after a period of time, another squad broke radio silence and told me that they thought they were not watching a good spot! I told them they were watching a good spot! Shortly after that conversation they called me back and said they had almost hit a deer! An hour later, they called because they had backed over a sharp rock and gotten a flat tire and need help changing it. While helping them with their tire, a vehicle shined a field ¾ of a mile down the road. There was no way to get to it. I was getting angry.

The night was about ruined, but not over yet.

I was about ready to call it a night, when my new supervisor called. They needed an extra spare. You guessed it, he had told Bob to drive unto the field so they could see if they had any bait (deer). They got unto the field and found out they had two flat tires! Remember, I had shown him and told him not to drive on the field that afternoon! My partner and I arrived. I called my supervisor every name in the book. Stupid, dumb and others I won't mention. Bob just stood there and didn't say a thing. It wasn't his fault and he knew I had every right to rant. My supervisor said that they had set their tire wrench down in the tall alfalfa and couldn't find it. I reached down in the alfalfa next to one of the flats and came up with their tire iron. More ranting and raving. We got their tires changed and everyone went home.

The next day the farmer called me and told me that spiking the field didn't work. He said someone had driven right over it and just bent the nails over. I told him it did work, he caught my dumb supervisor!

6

SMELT RUN

When I arrived in the Willow River station in Pine County, Minnesota, I learned that my station contained a unique lake-Grindstone Lake-located west of the town of Sandstone.

Grindstone is a very deep lake (151'). Fisheries had managed it for trout for many years. It has had special regulations for many years. It was stocked with brown, lake and I think rainbow trout. It also contained smelt. No one knows how the smelt got into the lake. Fisheries denies putting them in for the trout to feed on.

Every spring we would have a smelt run on Grindstone. They would run up the creek at the public access, the creek on the Audubon property and some would even go down the outlet (Grindstone River) a short ways. This smelt run attracted a lot of attention from fishermen who wanted to dip some of the fine eating little fish.

The Audubon did not want smelters on their property and posted it with "No Trespassing" signs. Smelting usually took place after dark and people would leave a mess of garbage up and down the creek. The public access creek was usually packed full of people, so individuals would sneak unto the Audubon property. This created a large trespass problem.

April 12, 1977, I got a call from the people at the Audubon Center that they had trespassers on their property that would not leave. I figured that I would need some help, so I contacted my neighboring officer to give me a hand. We arrived at the Audubon property shortly after midnight. We met with the individual who had called me with the trespassing complaint. He described the individuals (two men and one women). He had asked them to leave, but they had refused. They did leave when he told them he was going to call the warden.

My partner and myself went over to the public access to check on the smelting activity and see if the trespassers had went over there to try their luck. There were lots of people there after smelt! After checking a few fishing licenses, I noticed three individuals matching the description of the trespassers on the Audubon property.

We approached the individuals, I identified ourselves and asked them if they had been on the Audubon property earlier that night. They admitted that they had been there. I asked them for some identification. The two men gave me their driver licenses. I asked the women for her identification.

The second man (her boyfriend) told her, "you don't have to give them any I.D." She said that it was alright and handed me her drivers license. Her boyfriend grabbed her license from me during the exchange and backed off. He then took off his jacket and said, "Let's go" to me! He then approached me with clinched fist. As I prepared to defend myself, he kicked me in the groin area! My partner then stepped in and said to the individual, "Now hold it just a minute." The individual then kicked at my partners groin area! My partner turned and was gone. The individual then turned to me again. I just happened to have my heavy-duty, aircraft aluminum Kel-light in my hand. I extended my arm and whacked him right between the eyes. He didn't go down, but he did start backing up with me following him. I thought the creek would stop him, but he entered the creek and backed across and disappeared into the alder brush. I was left standing there, but I had his drivers license! I wanted this guy bad, but first I had to find my partner. I found him back at the squad. I asked him why he had left. He told me he had went to call for backup! I thought he was my backup! I told him to stay with the other two while I went looking for the groin kicker.

I knew the individual was in the narrow strip of brush between the lake and the road. I very quietly and slowly walked the road in the dark. It was a quite night, so I stopped and listened often. It was only a matter of time and he'd come back to the road and I'd have him. After a short time a vehicle came out of the public access and turned toward me. I stepped off the road into the edge of the brush to let the car pass me. A hundred yards down from me the cars brake lights came on-it stopped! Out of the brush came an individual and got into the car and it sped away. My perpetrator had gotten away-for now! I hustled back to the access and there was my partner without the two individuals I had told him to hold! I told him what had happened and asked him why he had let them go. He told me that he didn't think he had the right to hold them. I wasn't happy!

The individual had a Pine City address, so we went there that night. At first no one would answer the door, but after giving the door a severe beating, the girlfriend came to the door. I told her that I wanted to see her boyfriend NOW! She told me that he wasn't home. I believe that he was hiding in a back room, but we didn't have a warrant so we left.

I swore out a complaint on the individual and issued a ticket to the other two people involved. The groin kicker got a $100 fine for trespass and a $100 fine for simple assault. The other two got $25 fines each for trespass.

My supervisor, Ray Sanbeck, asked me how hard I had hit him. I told him that I tried to put him down!

7

SNOWMOBILE ASSAULT

I was working snowmobile enforcement one evening between Austin and Lansing, Minnesota, with my neighboring warden. We were encountering a few violations-mostly no registration on the snowmobiles. We had stopped a snowmobile in the ditch to check his registration (which he didn't have), when a snowmobile flew by us right down the middle of the paved county road! A serious safety violation. My partner pulled our snowmobile off the trailer and took off after the violator. I was writing a ticket to the individual with the unregistered machine, when I observed a snowmobile coming down the middle of the road from the direction my partner and violator had gone. I stepped out of my squad with my large flashlight in hand. I figured if he didn't want to stop, I'd take him right off his sled and end the illegal activity. The sled saw me and stopped. It was my partner and was he wild! He told me to drop everything and come with him. I told him no, I was going to finish up with what I had and then we'd see about the other violator.

When I was finished I asked my partner what had happened. He told me he had tracked the violator into his yard and when he had approached him about the violation the violator had assaulted him! I asked him how he was assaulted. My partner said the man had pushed him. I asked my partner if he had pushed him back. My partner said no, that's when he came back to get me to help him! We work alone on the job most of the time and I couldn't really understand why my partner hadn't taken care of the violation.

We loaded our snowmobile and went to the residence in Lansing where the alleged assault had taken place. We went to the door and knocked. A lady came to the door, and seeing our uniforms said that we had better be careful coming unto private property! I guessed we had the right place! I asked to see the man of the house. A male voice from another room out of our sight said, "Tell them to come back when they have a warrant!" Now I knew we had the right place! Not having a warrant and not in hot pursuit, we left.

I was able to get the guys name and address, but my partner would not be able to put a face with the name, so no warrant could be issued. I had another plan. I found out the guy worked at Hormel in Austin. I went to his place of work. I was able to talk with his supervisor and explain what happened. The violator did not want to talk or see me. I convinced his supervisor that I was there to get this misdemeanor violation of operating a snowmobile on a county road taken care of and behind us. His supervisor talked him into talking with me. The man and his supervisor sat down with me. I explained to the individual that I was not going to pursue the assault charge, if he would take a ticket from me for running on the road. I did explain that if he would not accept this then my partner and I would have to sit outside his house, so my partner could identify him. Then a warrant would be issued. I also told him that the cost of the warrant would more than likely be added to his fine upon conviction. He accepted a summons from me. He paid a fine of $25. I suppose that was a lot of money in 1974!

8

EXCUSES, EXCUSES, EXCUSES !

When individuals are caught in a violation, many of them just have to come up with an excuse as to why they did what they did. It would seem easier to just say, "You got me." Some individuals did say just that! The following are some excuses violators told me to explain their actions. Many of them have been heard by generations of Game Wardens and some of them are unique.

Fishermen by nature are prone to making up stories. The size, number and where the fish are caught are all suspect when talking to fishermen and fisherwomen! Some of the best excuses I heard were from fishermen who left their lines unattended, usually off of docks. One of the most common excuses for having an unattended line was to blame it on one of the kids in the cabin. This excuse didn't work with me when the reel was a spinning reel with the bail open and the lure was a floating jig with a leech on it. Definitely not a kids setup! One individual, with a line off the dock, was later found and questioned as to where he was, told me that he had gone to town to get some ice cream. Some other good excuses for an unattended line were: I just went up to the cabin to get some breakfast, I had to go to the bathroom, and I went to change my socks! I always asked them why they hadn't pulled up their line before doing these things. No one had a good answer for that other than, "I forgot."

A lot of men and women had excuses for not buying a fishing license. One excuse that was believable, but did not get the individual out of a ticket, was the excuse that fishing had not been a planned event. A spur of the moment decision to go fishing was made when the opportunity arose. I checked a lady fishing one day and asked her for her license. She told me that she didn't have one and that she really hadn't planned on fishing. It cost her a $44.00 fine.

Spearing northern pike through the ice requires a special license. I checked an individual in a dark house one day. The hole was open, a decoy was down and a spear was ready to go. I asked the individual for his spearing license. He told me that he wasn't spearing, he had just entered the house to warm up. He received a ticket.

One day, I checked an individual fishing without a license. The gentleman was from Indiana. He told me that he wasn't fishing, he was just reeling in the line to see if there was a fish on it! The fines had gone up. It cost him $50.00 for "not" fishing. Another individual fishing with a bobber and hook baited with a worm, told me that he was just trying out his new rod and reel. The fines kept going up. That one cost this guy $77.00. One of the best excuses for not having a fishing license was the guy who told me, "It's not like I was trying to catch anything."

The best excuse that didn't work for fishing with two lines in the summer happened when I checked an individual that I had observed fishing with two different lines for about 20 minutes. While watching him with binoculars, I observed him braking the line on his second rod and reel. He retied a new hook on it and re-baited it and put it back in the water. When I approached the individual and informed him that it was against the law to fish with two lines, he said, "Oh, is that one out?" He received a ticket after I explained to him that I had been watching him. The fine was $89.00 in 1992.

There were other excuses for doing things against the law while fishing. Not all the lakes in Minnesota have a public access. This does not mean that people are exempt from state law on these lakes. I caught a guy with an unattended line on one of these lakes. He thought it was a private lake and he didn't have to obey state laws. Wrong!

I checked a fisherman before opening of bass season one year. The individual had a couple of northern pike and a couple of bass. I informed him that bass season was not open yet. He told me that the only fish that he could identify were northern pike. I told him in that case he should have thrown all the fish back that weren't northern pike. He received a ticket for taking bass in closed season.

One night I was fishing on Sturgeon Lake with a friend. When fishing after sunset the law requires an anchored boat to have a white light displayed that can be seen from any direction. We were displaying a light. Any boat that was underway also needed a red and green light displayed on the front of the boat, plus the white light. It was well after sunset and very dark. All of a sudden a motor boat came screaming by us with no lights on what so ever! I turned to my friend and said let's get 'em! I always carried a ticket book with me even when I wasn't working-just in case! We were able to follow the boat by it's wake. I was hollering for him to stop and that I was a Conservation Officer. He finally stopped. I asked him what in the name of Sam Hill (who is Sam Hill?) he was doing driving his boat wide open without lights on such a dark night. His excuses was his motor had quite just before dark and he had just gotten it restarted. I asked him, if that was the case, why wasn't he going really slow and hugging the shore line? He said that he thought by going as fast as he could he would be spending less time on the lake therefore being less likely to hit another boat! He got a ticket!

The hunting seasons also brought out some excuses. Some actually said that they forgot to buy license. The one that really bothered me was when they told me that they didn't know the gun was loaded in the motor vehicle! They always, except once, (truly an accident), got a ticket and a safety lesson for having a loaded firearm in/on a motor vehicle. One guy even told me that he didn't know that a firearm had to be in a case in a motor vehicle. He does now and it only cost him $50.00.

It was and still might be against the law to shine deer after 10:00 p.m. during certain times of the year even without a firearm or implement capable of taking a big game animal with you. One night I stopped a vehicle shining fields at 12:05 a.m. The driver's excuse was that he was just showing his wife the deer. I informed him that deer could be seen a lot earlier at night. It cost him $145.00. I did not give his wife a ticket too.

People even had excuses for not having their registration displayed on their boats or snowmobiles. One individual told me that he had been looking for a certain style "X" for over a year so he could match the one on his wife's snowmobile. He paid a $24 fine for not having his registration displayed.

Still the best ever excuse was when the deer shiner Bob and I caught, told Bob the reason he forgot he had a loaded firearm in the vehicle was that he had forgotten to take his memory pills!

9

NEWSPAPERS

Newspapers friend or foe? I guess I was lucky, I always considered newspapers as friends. They always printed articles that were favorable to me and the department of natural resources. Through these articles, I was able to inform and educate the public. I often gained information from reading newspapers.

One of my duties as a conservation officer was to enforce the rules and regulations on fires. One of these regulations was for allowing a fire to spread. Usually this entailed forestry discovering an illegal fire or a legal fire that got away. One such incident, a fire had gotten away from a burn barrel and forestry had to put it out. They usually called me to do the enforcement action. I determined what happened and issued the responsible party a summons.

The person that I issued the ticket to did not show up for court. A warrant was issued for his arrest. Some time later, I was reading the St. Paul paper and I saw a picture and article about the suspect. It was his obituary! The older you get the more you read the obituaries. This is to see if any people you knew had died and to make sure you weren't listed! I informed the court that they could dismiss the warrant and ticket.

Fire started by man in obituary!

Late one March, I was called to the home of the editor of our local paper. He had been burning in his burn barrel and the fire had spread to the grass around the barrel and to a 20 acre field on his property. Forestry personnel were there and put the fire out. I did my job and issued a ticket. The forestry personnel and myself were invited into Dave's home for some fresh bread and coffee (I don't drink coffee, but the bread was good!). Dave also wanted some words of wisdom to pass along to his readers. The next issue of the *Askov American* contained a nice editorial about what happened and the information we had given him on burning rules and regulations.

Burning illegal material.

Reading the *Askov American* one day, I came upon a picture of a young girl feeding a fawn deer. The caption said, "Feeding a Fawn is Fun." I got a hold of Dave immediately. I explained what was wrong with this picture. The next issue of the paper, the picture was repeated with the caption, "Feeding a Fawn is Fun-But Also Illegal." The picture also had a short article written by me explaining the ramifications of making pets of wild animals and what people should do if they "find" a fawn deer and are tempted to take it home.

I was called to a residence east of Askov about a buck deer that had a red bandana around it's neck. The deer was chasing the individual's young children around the yard. It obliviously had been someones pet they had raised from a fawn illegally. I was concerned for the safety of the children. While trying to decide what to do, the buck came up to me and lowered it's head and tried to gore me with it's horns! I grabbed it by the horn with my right hand and drew my revolver with my left hand and shot and killed the deer. I felt bad for the deer, it deserved a better fate. Dave once again did a nice article about why deer shouldn't be tamed. The department did not have tranquilizer guns available, so there was no alternative.

The newspaper also alerted me to violations that were taking place. A guest columnist wrote a column about his grandfather. He wrote about his grandfather's secret to fishing success. He gave a step-by-step account of his grandpa's secret fishing method.

1. Catch a large perch off the dock.

2. Get a large bamboo pole, strung with black, 30-lb. test nylon line, and equipped with a large hook, a large sinker and a large bobber.

3. Impale the large perch onto the large hook and, with a big sweep of the large pole, flip it as far away from the dock as possible.

4. Secure the pole to the dock. (hay barn rope or 3/8" cable will do)

5. Lie down on the couch inside the cabin and fall asleep.

6. When you wake up go and see if the large bobber is largely visible.

7a. If the bobber is visible, return to the couch.

7b. If the bobber is not found, set the hook, drag in the fish, and repeat steps 1-7.

I wrote a letter to the editor. I told the readers that grandpa's fishing secret was illegal. Not only was the line unattended, but he also was using game fish for bait! I knew where their cabin was and promised to watch it a lot closer. There was an added P.S. that Rob said a small sunfish works better! Dave added for me that any game fish was illegal for bait.

The best picture of a violation was of a father and his son riding on the front of a friend's jeep both with at least fully uncased firearms. I would bet they probably were loaded too. They were dressed in blaze orange for the color photo. The picture was in the St. Paul paper. Not a good safety message!

So, all present and future game wardens remember to read your newspapers, you never know what you will discover. Also, getting to know your editor will help you get information to the public. It wouldn't hurt for everyone else to read a newspaper to stay informed too.

10

DUCK HUNTERS

One fall, during duck season in 1980, I got a call that someone was chasing and shooting at ducks from a motor boat on one of my lakes. Arriving at the lake, I observed the individual operating his boat and shooting at ducks in open water. He was doing this well within 500 feet from a home without permission as required by law. I got his attention and had him come to shore. I checked his licenses and stamps. They were all in order. His firearm was plugged, but loaded and uncased. I then asked him where the duck was that I saw him shoot. He told me it was just one of those divers and no good to eat, so he left it on the lake. It turned out to be a hen mallard! When he figured out that he was getting some tickets for the violations that he had committed, his attitude went south. I wasn't very happy with him either. I issued him a ticket for wanton waste of one duck. He paid a fine of $25 for that violation. I issued him a ticket for having a loaded and uncased firearm in a motor vehicle. That violation cost him $50. He also got a ticket for hunting within 500 feet of an occupied home. A $100 fine. Lastly, I gave him a ticket for taking migratory waterfowl in open water. Another $100 fine. I let him keep his equipment. I think he learned a lot about duck hunting laws that day. I gave the duck to the individual who reported the violations.

Another duck season, I caught a hunter with three wood ducks. The limit was two, so he got a ticket for one over the limit. His fine was $135. Prices had gone up! What hurt him most was that I took all three ducks from him. He figured wrong that he should be able to keep the limit of two. I gave the three ducks to a very dear friend—Aggie. She really enjoyed wild game.

I had a small lake in the extreme northeastern part of my area. Black lake was partially in Wisconsin. I had seen the lake from the air. I heard that the lake was noted for it's goose hunting. Waterfowl hunters could only get to the lake from the Wisconsin side. I figured that we could surprise some hunters if we came into the lake from the Minnesota side. I thought that being so remote there was a good possibility for some violations. Black Lake is located east of the old town site of Harlis about a mile through some real tough bog. Harlis isn't even on the map any more. It is located about three miles north of the old town site of Belden on the old railroad grade. Neither town has been there for nearly 100 years.

After heading north to Harlis on the old railroad grade, my neighboring officer Pete Jensen and myself headed east.

We were using Pete's 12 foot boat and motor. He was writing them off on his taxes, so I didn't mind using his equipment. We followed a very small creek that flowed out of Black Lake. After some time and several small beaver dams, we made it to Black Lake. There were two different parties set up hunting the lake. It was the first (and last?) time they had ever seen Minnesota Game Wardens on the lake. All the hunters had Minnesota and Wisconsin licenses and duck stamps. They all had federal duck stamps too. All hunters were using steel shot. The firearms were all plugged to only hold three shells. There were no over limits either. That bunch of hunters were about the most legal guys I'd ever checked in such a remote area. One gentleman did have an unsigned federal duck stamp. I had him sign the stamp. I issued him a written warning only, so I had a record that we had been on Black Lake. We never went back. Black Lake is now part of the Black Lake Bog Scientific and Natural Area.

Poached mallards.

11

DOUBLE TROUBLE

Deer season does not always bring out the best in some individual hunters. It seems way to important to shoot a deer. Often deer would feed in fields along roadways offering to much temptation for road hunters. Road hunters are usually individuals who have no place to hunt or don't like to sit out in the cold. They drive around until they see a deer standing near the road. They then shoot from the road. If the deer falls, they load it into their vehicle and try to leave the area before they get caught. This type of "hunting" is what makes the deer decoys so effective.

One day early in the deer season, a local hunter was in his deer stand. He observed an individual shoot from his vehicle on the county road at a deer in a hay field. The shooter then drove onto the field and finished the buck fawn. The hunter got out of his stand and confronted the poacher. (not always a good idea) The poacher was informed that he was on private property. The poacher told the hunter that he was handicapped and could hunt where ever he wanted to hunt. The hunter took down the license number of the vehicle and contacted me. I ran the license number and it came back to an individual from the twin cities. The description the hunter gave me of the vehicle matched the information I got back on the motor vehicle. The hunter was also willing to identify the poacher and testify in court. With this information, I sent the poacher a ticket for shooting a big game animal from the roadway. I also sent him a warning ticket for trespassing on agricultural land.

One week later, still in deer season, I received another complaint about the same individual doing the same thing. He was caught by the landowner shooting at a deer from a county road unto the landowners hay field. This happened in another part of my patrol area. This guy really got around! I sent him another ticket for shooting at a big game animal from the roadway. I also sent him another warning ticket for trespassing on agricultural land.

With the courts help, I finally did get the poachers attention. The case was set for a pre-trial hearing. The county attorney requested that I interview the suspect. In the taped interview, the suspect admitted shooting at the deer, but stated that he had driven down into the ditch first. The suspect did have a handicapped permit that allowed him to shoot from a standing, non-running motor vehicle. This permit does not allow an individual to shoot from a roadway or trespass. The ditch was very steep and had a fence at the bottom, so I didn't really believe him. Also, the ditch is part of the road right of way. My witnesses were going to all testify that he had shot from the road.

Finally, nearly a year later, the poacher pled guilty through a plea negotiation. He received a fine of $200 plus 30 days in jail. The jail time was stayed for one year. That meant that if he didn't get caught within one year doing the same sort of violation, he wouldn't have to spend 30 days in jail. He didn't get caught within that year. I hope he changed his ways of hunting.

12

SMALL GAME

As a Conservation Officer, I had lots of contacts with small game and small game hunters. In my first station, Austin, Minnesota, protected and unprotected animals would be cause for complaints. I would do my best to help people out with their complaints.

On night, I wound up chasing a gray squirrel around in an elderly ladies unfinished attic. The only weapon that I could think of to safely use in the attic was a fish spear. I also had to be careful not to step between the ceiling joist. If I had made a misstep, I would have wound up in her living room! I did finally subdue the critter to the delight of the lady. I told her to have the holes in her eaves plugged, to prevent squirrels from getting in again.

Helping out almost got me into trouble one day. I had purchased a pellet gun to take care of any pest in town, that being much safer then a regular firearm. A lady called and complained about a rabbit eating all her flowers. I went and investigated. Sure enough, the little bugger had eaten all her flowers right down to the ground. I spotted the plump culprit, and dispatched it. I felt pretty good about solving her problem, until she called me a week later. She had another rabbit eating her flowers! What had I started? I shot the second rabbit, but it made it to the neighbors yard before it died. I walked over to pick it up and the neighbor lady came screaming out her back door! This second lady had dishes of food out feeding the rabbits. She threatened to call the SPCA, my boss and the governor. I had to do some fast, sweet talking. I was able to stay out of trouble by explaining why I had shot the rabbit. From then on, I told people to fence their flowers and gardens.

Another time, I dispatched a woodchuck who was destroying another garden. I carried the critter up to the house to show the lady that I had accomplished my mission. When she opened the door and saw what I had, she covered her eyes and said, "Don't show it to me, I'll cry." I just shook my head and left.

When I moved to Willow River, Minnesota, these type of complaints stopped. People in smaller towns knew what to do about these problems. I now had more problems with the hunters of small game.

One day I was bow hunting on private property with the permission of the landowner. I was settled into my tree stand, when I noticed two hunters walking in the woods in my direction. I was sure that I was the only individual who had permission to hunt that property. Both individuals were carrying shotguns. Not noticing me, they walked right under my stand. I asked them what they were doing. After the initial start, they said that they were grouse hunting. They apologized for messing up my hunt and left. They seemed to recognize me and were very nervous. I decided to get down and follow them back to their truck and check their hunting licenses. One of

Grouse on the hood of my truck inside the garage.

the hunters did not have a license and I issued him a ticket. I always had a ticket book with me! The wooded land wasn't posted, so I didn't issue any tickets for trespassing. I did tell them to always get permission on private land. Talk about bad luck, for them to have walked up on a game warden sitting in a tree, in the middle of the woods. The individual paid a $40.00 fine in 1980.

One fall, the week before raccoon season, I was out looking for hunters getting a jump on the season. I came upon a car parked along a lonely back road at 1:00 a.m. I checked it out. No one was in the vehicle. It looked like they were hunters, because the vehicle contained an empty gun case. I listened and could hear coon hounds baying in the woods. I hid my squad and needed a place to hide near the vehicle while I waited for the hunters to come out of the woods. It was a cold night, so I decided to hide in the suspect's car. I hunkered down in the front seat on the drivers side. When the illegal hunters returned, they opened the back door of their car and let the coon hound jump in. The dog peeked over the front seat and sniffed me. I'm glad it wasn't a mean dog! The driver opened the front door and there I was.

The individuals (a guy and his girlfriend) had taken one raccoon. Neither individual had any identification with them. I radioed my neighboring conservation officer to come and assist me with taking them to jail. Without identification, they could have given us a false name and address and it would have been difficult to find them once we let them go. Each individual was given a ticket for taking/possessing one raccoon during closed season. I also seized a .357 handgun, a .22 rifle, a couple lights, a hunting knife and one raccoon. They sat in jail for 36 hours, before they could see a judge. The reason for the long wait was that it was a weekend and judges don't work on weekends. The judge found them guilty and gave them the 36 hours in jail as the fine. I did confiscate all the articles that I had seized.

Beaver cut aspen that hit a power line, causing a wildfire.

13

FISH RUN

Every spring northern pike, walleye and suckers swim up stream to spawn. This leaves them very vulnerable to poachers. People would wade the small streams and take the spawning fish with dip nets or spears. Suckers could be taken during daylight hours usually after May 1st, unless the stream was closed because of a late spring run of fish.

One spring, the last day of April, my neighboring officer and myself were heading to Mille Lacs Lake. Mille Lacs had a huge fish run, and the neighboring officers were always available to help. On the way to Mille Lacs, I wanted to stop and check one of my creeks for activity. It was well after dark when we got to the vicinity of the creek. We found a truck parked off the road in an old wooded over field, within walking distance of the creek. I told my partner that we had people on the creek. Sometimes these people would just be looking at the fish and other times they would be trying to get the fish! We hid our squad within sight of the truck and waited. After a period of time, three individuals came back to the truck from the creek. We waited until they were in the truck and moving before we stopped them. They had a couple of five gallon pails with fish in them! They only had dip nets with them, no spears. The individuals were three older men from the area. One was quite talkative. He tried to explain to me that they only had suckers and that the fish dropped back into the lake during daylight hours and were unavailable then. After dark, Game Wardens have to be very stern and be in control of the situations. I told them in very strong terms, that what they had done was wrong and that I had better not find any northern pike or walleyes in their pails. I dumped their pails out on the ground. They only had suckers. I told them that I was letting them off with a warning. I also told them, that if they had had spears or game fish it would have been a different story. One of the individuals, who hadn't said one word was shaking. I asked him what was wrong? He said, "I'm to scared to talk." We let them keep the suckers and left for Mille Lacs.

One spring, I was checking a creek in my area for fish run activity. I noticed five little holes in the road by the creek. Looking further, I noticed five holes in a row every so often. The light bulb came on. Some one had been walking by the creek with a five tined spear. Every so often, the individual would use the spear like a cane leaving the five little holes in a row! There was most likely only one place the spearer could have come from, the nearest farmstead. I went and talked with the farmer. We had a good conversation like we always had had. I brought up what I had observed by the creek and asked him if he had any ideas who might be trying to take fish. He just looked at me for a second. He then told me that his boys had been down there. He told me that he thought it was okay because the creek only had suckers in it. I told him the boys could only spear suckers in daylight hours after May 1st. Ed became a very good friend and raised a number of fawns for me. He's gone now, and I miss him.

The middle of April, 1980, my neighboring warden Bob Kangas and my self had a good stretch of luck catching fish poachers. We were working a small creek west of Finlayson. The first night, a little after 11:00 p.m., we caught two individuals spearing northern pike. They each paid $200 in fines. Three nights later, we caught three more locals with spears on the same creek at about the same time. They had no fish so they all paid only $100 in fines. After that the word was out that we were watching that creek. We caught no one else there that spring.

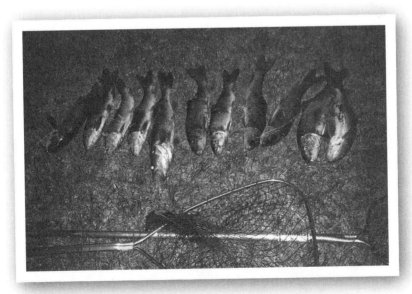

Fish taken illegally during spring fish run.

14

BREAKS

My job as a Conservation Officer allowed me to write a ticket for a violation or not write one. Each encounter with an individual who was violating a law was decided on its own merits. Most cases if I could determine the person unknowingly violated a law, I would use the opportunity to educated and inform the individual. I always believed that if I could gain compliance of the law, without writing a ticket, I had done my job. Also, some times the violation was minor and really didn't impact the resource. The attitude of the individual also was important. Later in my career the state came up with warning tickets. This was a very useful tool. It let our supervisors know we were working and it didn't cost the individual any money!

Deer season provided a lot of opportunities for tickets, both regular and warning, and opportunities to give people breaks.

One deer season I was patrolling east of a town in my area. I came upon four ladies all dressed in blaze orange lined up on the road. None of them were carrying firearms. I stopped and asked what they were up to. They told me that they were getting ready to make a deer drive for their husbands that were on stand at the other end of the wooded area. I asked them if they had deer licenses. None of them did. I informed them that they needed licenses to assist in the taking of deer. They were unaware of that. I issued no tickets. The next year they were in the same spot. Guess what, they all had licenses! I had to give them a little bit of a hard time and suggested that they should be on stand and their husbands should be making a drive for them! I felt I had done my job.

The law on tagging deer used to be the deer had to be tagged before bring it into camp or before placing it on a motor vehicle. Now it has to be tagged at the site of kill. I think the purpose of the law was so unethical hunters wouldn't sneak deer home, not use their tag and go out and get another deer. I think there is less of that now with all the bonus deer licenses available. I did catch hunters with untagged deer trying to sneak them home. Often times one hunter would be riding in the back of the truck ready to slip the tag on if they were stopped by Game Wardens. Usually we were to quick for them! They would also lose their deer in that case.

I was checking for hunting activity down a dead end road one day. At the end of the road sat a pickup with one very tired and happy hunter. He had shot a large ten point buck and had just finished loading it by himself in the back of his pickup.

I knew the hunter and checked his license. I then said, do you think it's time to tag your deer? He looked at me with his mouth open. He had forgotten to tag his buck! I allowed him to tag it and didn't give him a ticket. He was even happier.

I wrote a lot of tickets for uncased and/or loaded firearms in motor vehicles. Other than the one time the 30-30 cartridge was stuck in the magazine unknown to the hunter, I always wrote a hard ticket if the firearm was loaded. I felt the safety issue was justifiable enough even if the person truly was unaware. The issue of an uncased firearm was a different story. The law says that it has to be completely enclosed, and the case has to be fully zipped, snapped, buckled or tied. Also, it had to be in a case made for a firearm. The firearm could be in the trunk of a car uncased with the trunk door closed. I also told hunters that no one could be riding in the trunk with the firearm! Some people thought if you broke the gun down that it was okay to transport it that way. They would have a double barreled shotgun in three pieces on the back seat. I would have to tell them no, that was never a law. That would get them a written warning. One individual had his unloaded firearm wrapped in a blanket on the back seat. I asked to see his firearm and he told me that was where it was! I told him the law and had him put the firearm in the trunk of his car. No ticket was issued.

The height of deer stands was not something I choose to enforce. When I first started as a Conservation Officer the legal height for a stand was six feet. It then went to nine feet and then to sixteen feet! Portable stands can be any height. I'm glad I didn't write a bunch of tickets for over six feet. I was in the woods of an individual who became a very dear friend to look at something on his property with him. We drove on his trails and I noticed deer stands that were 12-14 feet in height.

At that time the law was six feet. I asked him if they were his stands. He looked up at them and said, yes, and in the same breath he said, "Boy, those trees really grew in a year!" I just laughed. It wasn't deer season and no one was in the stands so there was no violation. I wouldn't have written him a ticket anyway.

I did once threaten to write a ticket for a deer stand too high. I had a complaint that a neighbor had a very high stand on the property line over looking the complainant's hay field. I went out and looked at the stand. It was over 20 feet high! I went and talked to the stand's owner. He stated that it wasn't a deer stand, it was a tree house! He must have thought I had just fallen off the turnip truck! I told him that if on opening day, someone was in his tree house with a rifle, they were getting a ticket for a deer stand that was too high. I also suggested that he take down the stand because it only looked unto his neighbor's property and he did not have permission to hunt there. He was not happy! I did go back during the deer season and the "tree house" was no longer there.

At one time trappers had the option of bringing furs to tag to the game warden. I tagged many critters on the floor of my wife's kitchen! Bless her heart for putting up with that and all the other things. A young man and his dad brought me a fisher to tag one year. He also had a mink that he wanted to turn in. He had caught it the day after mink season closed! I looked at him and thought now there is a honest young man! I asked him if he had caught any other mink that season. He said that he had. I told him to take the mink home and put it with the rest of his catch. I think that was a good reward for being honest.

One spring I went over to an old trapper's home to pick up an otter that he had accidentally caught in a beaver set. He always called me when that happened. When I got to his place, I couldn't help but notice a fresh northern pike skin and backbone lying in his yard. Since it wasn't open season for northerns yet, I asked him about the remains. He told me that he had caught it in a conibear trap set for beaver and he wasn't going to let it go to waste, so he brought it home and ate it! I looked him in the eye and told him that was illegal because season wasn't open and a trap is an illegal means for taking fish. I told him that I wasn't always going to be around. I told him the next Game Warden might not understand and give him a ticket. I told him next time to call me and I would give him a permit to keep the fish to eat. He, like I, couldn't bear to see anything go to waste. There was no intent to violate or he wouldn't have left the remains where I could see them. No ticket was issued.

Once in awhile some thing gets shot that shouldn't. I observed three duck hunters heading toward the landing on one of my lakes. I timed it right and was standing at the landing just as three duck hunters in a canoe approached. The hunter in the center of the canoe was a young girl. The other two hunters were young guys. As they neared the landing they could see that I was a Conservation Officer. The young girl proudly held up a bird and proclaimed, "I got my first duck!" When they got to the landing she asked me if I could identify it for her. I could. I told her it was a pied-billed grebe. I asked her if it had swam into the decoys and if she had shot it on the water. She said that is what happened. I had to inform them that the grebe is a federally protected bird and that it was illegal to kill it. They had no clue. I admonished the three young hunters for not knowing what they had shot. I told them that I had to take the grebe, but was letting them off with a warning. They thanked me and assured me that it would never happen again.

Another time I checked some young hunters just leaving a duck blind. All was in order. Just after they left I noticed something floating on the water. I got a long stick and was able to fish it out. It was a belted king fisher! I hurried and caught up with the hunters just before they got to their truck. I confronted them with the evidence. One young hunter admitted that he had shot the bird thinking it was a duck as it passed over their decoys. It was a wooded situation, so there wasn't much time it identify it. The individual was given a warning because of his age and he had admitted his mistake. The king fisher was mounted by the taxidermy students at Pine City Technical College and given to Willow River High School for a teaching aid.

Adults also made mistakes. One non-resident bear hunter couldn't wait to show me the bear he had shot. It was in a refrigerator in a black plastic bag. When I looked inside the refrigerator I asked if it was only the hide in the bag. He said it was the whole bear! Upon further examination, I determined that it was a cub. I had to inform him of that and that cubs were not legal. He had never even seen a bear in the wild. It just looked big to him! My area was in the no quota area and the wildlife folks didn't care how many bear were shot there. The individual was let off with a warning.

There were lots of opportunities to give breaks to fishermen. We used to be able to enter a fish house unannounced to check for illegal activity. That is why there is a law saying that the door can not be locked. Checking fishermen one night by myself on Mille Lacs Lake, I came upon a house that appeared to be occupied. I went to the door but it was locked! I banged on the door and said, "Game Warden, open up!" A voice from inside said, "Just a minute." After I gained entrance to the house I looked around and observed only four holes each with one line down. I checked the elderly couple's licenses and told them that it was illegal to have the door locked. The man said that they were afraid and that is why they kept their door locked at night after they went to bed. I could understand their reason for having the door locked and they had no other violations, so I told them to have a good night and left.

Another time I spotted an individual casting off the dam on Big Pine Lake. It was prior to the northern/walleye opener. I stopped to check his license. He didn't have one, he said he was just trying out his new rod and reel. He was casting a spoon with treble hooks on it. From the looks of things I believed him. I showed him how he could still practice without getting into trouble. I took his lure and removed the hooks by undoing the "O" ring. No ticket was issued.

I checked a fisherman who had 32 sunfish-two over the limit at that time. He had lost count. I picked out the two biggest sunfish and threw them back into the lake. I told the fisherman that he was all done and should go home. He did.

Pete and I watched a lone fisherman on a small lake in his area with binoculars. He had a bunch of crappie on the ice. We observed him putting something under a snow pile. Time to check this guy out! When we arrived out on the lake the fisherman had exactly fifteen crappie on the ice. A limit. I kicked around in the snow pile near him and discovered an extra real nice crappie. He did not receive a warning!

An individual caught a nice northern pike on opening day. He took the seven pound fish into the sport shop to get weighed. When the employee at the sport shop saw the fish, all he said was, You'd better go see Curt! The lake had been stocked with muskie and the fisherman didn't know a musky from a northern. He had caught a small muskie. He called me up and brought the fish over to my house. He felt real foolish.

I took the fish and let him off with a warning. I destroyed the fish and understand it tasted real good!

I stopped out at a hunting camp one day. There in the yard sat two new ATV's. The hunters were proud of their new purchases. I asked them if they had gotten them registered. They just stopped and looked at me. They did not know they had to be registered! The very next week the machines were registered. These same individuals liked to wear hand guns around their property. One individual was about to get on his ATV with his hand gun on his hip. I stopped him and asked if he had a permit to carry a loaded handgun on a motor vehicle. He didn't know what I was talking about. So, I explained. The next week he had his permit to carry.

When I was at a public access and saw a boat come in on a trailer that didn't have current registration on it, I always approached the owner and questioned his registration. Some times they had the paper work in their pocket. Sometimes they had their sticker with them, but hadn't put it on yet. In that case, I helped them get it on before launching their boat. If the boat wasn't currently registered I advised them not to put the boat in the water or I would have to give them a ticket. Some left happy and others were unhappy that they had come all that way and couldn't go fishing. I hope they were unhappy with themselves and not me!

These examples are not all that I gave a break to and a lot of knowing violators didn't get breaks!

15

TRAPPER CAUGHT

November 4th, 1987, I was informed by a local resident that there was a live raccoon in a trap near his residence. He later told me that he had also seen it on the 2nd and 3rd. On November 5th I had the informant show me the raccoon. It was still there, now sitting in the river. I killed the raccoon and left it in the water. It could be seen from the road. I returned the next day to find the animal still dead in the trap. I seized the raccoon, trap and stake. I issued the owner of the trap, identified by the required trap tag, a ticket for failure to tend a trap daily if the trap is not capable of drowning the animal. The animal must also be killed and removed from the trap. It cannot be killed and left in the trap by the trapper. I left it for the trapper to pick up if he returned to check his trap within the legal time limits. The reason for this law is obvious.

The trapper plead not guilty on December, 1987. Jury trial was set for May, 1988. I felt we had a good case. The trapper lived 150 miles from where he was trapping, he was a long liner. I believe that he may have just missed this one trap, but that doesn't eliminate his responsibility.

His lawyer did the best job he could. He rescheduled the trial for August, 1988. His lawyer wrote the county attorney a letter in April saying that his client had talked to his local DNR officer as well as the former president of the Minnesota Trappers Association. They told the trapper that my identification would be almost impossible without a tag or mark placed on the animal. I know now that I should have put something, such as a coin, in the animal after I killed it, but I still felt I had a good case. I found out later that the trapper was big in the trappers organization and needed badly not to have this conviction on his record. The lawyer also suggested that the trapper would be willing to pay the $110.00 fine if the conviction was not on his record. The trial was rescheduled for November, 1988.

The county attorney received another letter from the defense attorney in July before the November court date. In his letter he suggested how the trap checking played out. He suggested that the trapper was there every day at times when I wasn't there and that a new raccoon got caught and removed every day. Nice try.

In November, 1988, before the trial date the county attorney received another letter from the defense attorney stating that he had contacted a state game manager (later learned, fur specialist for the trapping association) who was going to testify about my incorrect identification procedures. Again he suggested the payment of the fine with no guilty finding. The trial was again rescheduled for the end of December, 1988.

An omnibus hearing was held early December, 1988. My witness and myself were questioned as to the facts. The trial was again rescheduled for February 1989. A plea bargain was reached mid January 1989. The defendant paid $110.00 court cost with no guilty plea. The raccoon was sold for the state for $18.00. The trap and stake were confiscated.

Raccoon illegally trapped.

16

WE NEED THE MEAT

Early November 1979, I received a call from my neighboring warden, Bob Kangas. He told me he had received information that a couple of guys had been seen shooting deer before the season. He asked if I'd be willing to help catch the individuals. Of course, I wasn't going to pass up the chance to catch some poachers!

I met Bob, who had gotten a search warrant.

Arriving at the residence of the suspected poacher, we noticed a small child in the yard. When we got out of the squad, I asked the young boy (about six years old) if his dad had any deer. The boy said yes, there is one hanging in the garage! The young always tell the truth! The wife of the suspect came out of the house. We asked to look at the deer in the garage. She said the door was locked and she didn't have the key. Our little helper stepped up to the plate and said, "Mommy, the key is hanging right there." The mom got red in the face. She was given a copy of the search warrant. She opened the garage and there hung a deer that had been gutted and skinned. The deer was not tagged and was covered with a brown jacket. We seized the deer plus 69 packages of meat from the freezer marked "deer." We also seized one buck fawn head, three deer hides and an unused 1979 bow and arrow deer tag.

Bob gave the lady the Miranda warning and took a statement from her. In her statement she told us the deer in the garage had been shot. She told us her husband and hunting companion (who she named) had left for the twin cities earlier that day. She also told us that deer that they got were always taken over to her husband's dad's place for final cutting and wrapping. Her husband's dad lived just down the road a mile or two. We thanked her and advised her not to call her father-in-law, because if she did she would be charged with interfering with an officer.

After leaving, Bob called the sheriff's office and gave the information to a deputy to get a search warrant for us for the father's place. We waited in sight of the residence, but out of sight!

The new search warrant arrived. We went to the residence and contacted the owner. He was not happy when Bob gave him the search warrant. I got to look through their large chest freezer while Bob kept an eye on the new suspect. The suspect's wife was wailing away while I was digging through her freezer. I came up with 82 packages marked "deer." We also seized one deer hide, some deer bones, a sheet of plastic

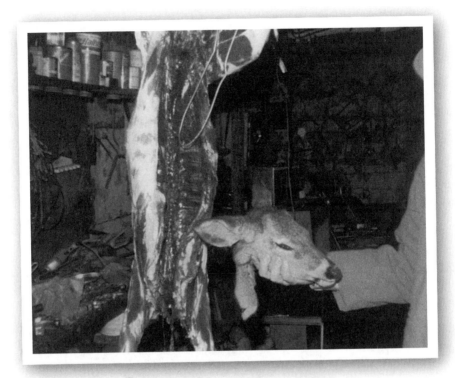

Deer found in garage, poached.

with blood on it, one broad head from a broken arrow with hair (deer) on it, a cardboard box with numerous fresh animal bones and a meat saw with hair and blood on the blade.

I'll never forget what the landowner said with his herd of beef cattle in the background, "Some of us need the meat to survive." His wife also worked for the state!

Bob followed up with the hunting companion. They were all charged with the illegal possession of five deer. I believe the fine was $150 for each deer, plus loss of their hunting privileges.

Poached deer-only back straps taken.

17

CHICKEN TICKETS

What is a chicken ticket? It could be a ticket that an officer would never write, or it could be one your neighboring officer always writes! Sometimes it may not have even been a violation of the law and a ticket was written.

As I see it, there are three reasons for writing this sort of ticket. One is that some officers get caught up in the numbers game. One of the things officers get evaluated on are the number of tickets that they write. These evaluations may lead to promotions and/or awards. The second reason is some officers believe that there is no gray area. You are either right or wrong. I had a much older officer tell me early in my career that everyone is a violator and it is up to us to catch them! What a scary thought. I developed the philosophy that 98% of the people are good (thank goodness for that), but I always knew that every once in awhile someone in that 98% might slip up and make a mistake, but that still didn't make them a bad person. The last reason is that some individuals just tick off the officer and the officer feels that he has to write him up for something. I don't blame the supervising officers (unless they are pushing for more tickets) because the details of the arrest are not always on the ticket, just the law violated. Example: the deer stand was above the height required by law, not that it was only one inch too high. Although, my older and wiser former neighboring officer Jim Bryant, says a good supervisor should know the kinds of tickets his/her officers are writing!

The following examples are tickets that I heard about or saw written, but would have never written myself.

I worked with an officer for one day during my training period. My regular training officer had personal business so he had me work with this officer. It was ruffed grouse season. We came upon an individual with his car parked at the end of a dead end trail. The drivers door was open. The individual had his shotgun lying on the seat of the car. The individual was several steps away from the car relieving himself. It sure looked to me like he had placed the shotgun on the seat to keep it safe while he attended to his other business. The officer I was working with gave him a ticket for transporting a loaded firearm in an automobile. After we left the individual, even though I was on probation (not good to tick off the training officer!), I protested the arrest as not being right. I said the individual had just laid his shotgun on the seat while he was relieving himself. Also the car was parked and not running and he was just going to pick up his gun and go hiking after grouse when he was done. The officer I was training with said there was an attorney general's opinion stating that the putting in or taking out constitutes transporting. I still protested. The officer took me to his residence and showed me in the law book the attorney general's opinion. I still didn't like the arrest. I later found out the opinion was written during prohibition when there was a problem with transporting illegal whiskey. Like my friend likes to put it, "The whiskey's in the car."

When I first came on the job the legal height for a deer stand was six feet off the ground. Any thing higher was illegal. Early in my career I was riding with a much older officer, when he pointed out a deer stand in his area that we could see from the road. The officer, my neighbor, stated that he was going to get someone in that deer stand on opening day. I asked him what for? He said, " It's six foot, two inches high, I measured it." I just sat there in quite disbelief. I later questioned the department why the law said six feet. I was told it was to protect the trees from damage. Having some knowledge of forestry, I said that didn't make sense as the first log in a tree is the money log (the one that is usually the most valuable). I was then told it was for safety reasons. I argued that the higher you went the more safe it would be as far as shooting goes. You would be shooting more into the ground, which would be a lot safer then shooting across an open 40 acre field. Also, you could sit on a limb as high as you wanted, but could not place a board on the limb to be more safe as far as falling out of the tree. The law was changed to nine feet and then later to sixteen feet. I chose not to write anyone for a deer stand too high in my whole career.

I watched the same officer give an individual a ticket for having his gun case unzipped one inch! He correctly quoted the law that says the case has to be completely zipped, snapped, buckled or tied with no portion of the firearm visible. I still thought the ticket was chicken, because, like Bob Kangas likes to say there was no furtive movement on the part of the driver.

An officer went to a new station and it appeared that he wanted to let the locals know a new, hard nosed warden was now in town. He went around a popular lake in his new area and hung a ticket on each boat that was unregistered and upside down on the shore. Watercraft have to be registered, but I am not sure they need to be when on shore and not being used. Another officer told me that when he saw an unregistered watercraft come onto an access he would wait and let them launch the watercraft before he approached them in hopes he could write a ticket. I would approach the individual with the watercraft that didn't appear to have current registration before they launched their boat and ask them about it. Sometimes they had renewed their registration and had the proper paper work. When they didn't I had to inform them that they could not put their boat in the water without getting a ticket. Some had just forgot and thanked me.

Fish houses when on lakes in the winter had to be licensed and have the name and address of the owner marked on the outside. Now you may have your drivers license number on the house. This was for identification incase the houses were left on the ice after they were supposed to be off the ice. This was a violation in of its self. The identification violation, if there was one, was no name or address on the fish house. Some officers would write a ticket if the owner had just left off his Zip Code! They justified the ticket by saying the Zip Code was part of their address.

When fishing in a fish house the door could not be locked. It had to be able to be opened from the outside. This was so the anglers in the house would not have time to pull up their extra lines or get rid of their illegal fish before letting the game warden in. One officer came up to a fish house and tried to jerk the door open. It slipped out of his hand and he had a hard time getting the door open. The angler had installed a very heavy spring to keep the door shut in high winds. The officer wrote him a ticket for having too tight of a spring on his fish house door!

Boat registration had to be displayed on the water craft in a certain location, size and spacing. I heard of an officer who carries a ruler and measures the spacing between the numbers and letters. If the spacing isn't as the boating synopsis states the boater gets a ticket. Canoes without motors didn't need the letters and numbers. I watched an officer give a couple canoeing a warning ticket for not having numbers on their canoe. I would have said something in their presence if it would have cost them money. After we departed I asked the officer what he was doing giving a warning ticket for something that wasn't a violation. He said he needed the pinch for his evaluation.

Trapping has lots of rules and regulations. The trapper has to have identification on each trap, so conservation officers can identify the owner if there is some problem. There is also a law saying a trap can not be set close to water before mink season. This law is to prevent the accidental take of mink before season. Another regulation on trapping is that body gripping traps of a certain size have to be only used in water with at least half the trap under water. This is so it is less likely to take a pet or a none targeted species. An individual asked a conservation officer in his area if he could set a live trap and catch a raccoon to let go to train his dog in trailing. The officer said he could. The next day the officer asked him where he had set the trap. The officer went and picked up the trap and gave the individual a ticket for no name and address on the trap and a warning ticket for trapping too close to water before mink season. Another officer gave a trapper a ticket for having his 330 conibear one inch too far out of the water. I also understand that officers have placed protected animals (dead) in traps to see if trappers are checking their traps in the time required. Entrapment? (pun intended)

My friend was hunting deer in Wisconsin. Wisconsin has a law that says you can not hunt from a permanent stand on state or county land. My friend was unaware of this law. He found an unoccupied stand on county land and climbed up in it. Along came the warden and gave him a ticket. (rightfully so) The warden then told him he could use the stand for the weekend. My friend thought that was awfully nice. The next day he went back and climbed into the stand. Along comes the same warden and issues him another ticket! This same warden is rumored to have moved county line signs to issue tickets because Wisconsin has different regulations for different counties.

Game birds have to have a wing, head and feet left on them after they are harvested for species and sex identification. I was working with an officer checking small game hunters when we came upon an individual with some game on the ground by his car. My partner immediately saw that they were completely dressed out. He informed the individual that this was against the law and he would have to give him a ticket. The individual said, "They changed the law on me again!" I just had to put a stop to this, I said, "(officers first name) they're squirrels!" The officer looked again, saw that they were indeed squirrels and told the individual that he could have them like that.

Another officer was in the habit of putting the deer decoy in the field across from the end of the driveway of a deer camp.

The decoy he used always had a big rack of horns. So when the hunters would drive out in the predawn of opening day their headlights would be on this big buck. The officer would take them for shinning deer and if they shot he also wrote them for taking in closed season because it was before hours on opening day.

I am against littering. I have made numerous littering cases, but this takes the cake in my opinion. A Wisconsin officer checked a duck hunter coming off a slough. The officer asked if he had any ducks, he didn't. The officer asked if he had shot. He said he did shoot, but missed. The officer then asked he see his empty shells. He said they went into the lake. He was given a ticket for littering. A Minnesota officer gave a duck hunter a litter ticket for picking the breast feathers off a duck and letting them float away on the water! What's next, will we have to account for all the pellets that aren't in our game?

There have been officers in the past and maybe even now who just aren't cut out for the job. They just don't like confrontations or giving people tickets. One officer retired for many years really disliked writing tickets. He still needed to produce even back then. He would look up a name and address in the phone book and write an inexpensive ticket and pay the fine to the court out of his own pocket! Another trick to get your numbers up is to go to cemeteries and get names and dates of birth and write warning tickets. I've never seen this done, but have heard that it may have been.

Life jackets are very important. Watercraft of certain sizes also have to have a throwable coast guard approved cushion or ring. An officer checked two anglers fishing in a 17 foot boat. Upon checking for life jackets he found that the two anglers had three life jackets, but no throwable. He issued the operator a ticket for no throwable device.

A friend of a friend was given a ticket for skating on thin ice on Lake Nokomis by a park board officer, not a game warden. The judge asked the officer just what he was doing bringing that into his court. The judge continued the case for dismissal.

These were or are in all probability very fine officers. One actually became officer of the year for the state of Minnesota!

Another became chief warden in another state! They probably wrote many very excellent tickets, but for some reason, these examples, in my opinion, where not their finest.

I am sure, some one can come up with tickets that I wrote that were chicken!

18

DEER SEASON

When November rolled around, I became very busy! Deer season was upon us in Northern Minnesota. Everyone seemed to be hunting deer. It also seemed that it was very important for these hunters to bag "their" deer. To some it didn't matter how they got the deer as long as they got one. Some of the violations I ran into were: loaded & uncased firearms, strung/uncased bows in/on motor vehicles, trespassing, shooting from roadways, untagged deer and baiting, shooting in closed hours and taking in closed areas.

Banning State Park was located in my patrol area. Unlike some state parks that had special deer hunts, Banning was not ever open for deer hunting. It did contain lots of deer. Banning State Park was bisected by State Highway 23. One deer season I came upon a vehicle parked along the highway with Banning State Park on both sides of the road. I stopped to see if someone was having trouble. No one was in the vehicle, but I did observe empty gun cases. It didn't matter which side of the road they were on-they were hunting in the park! I backed off and waited for the hunters to come out of the woods. After a time, here came three hunters walking out to their vehicle carrying firearms. I drove up to their vehicle just as they were walking out. They had walked right by a state park sign! I pointed the sign out to them and asked them what it said. They said, "state park." I told them that they couldn't hunt in the state park. One individual said that he heard that they could hunt in Itasca State Park, so they assumed they could hunt in this park. I informed them that Itasca State Park probably had a special hunt, but that didn't apply to this park. I issued both adults tickets for deer hunting in Banning State Park. The juvenile was given a warning ticket. After having them sign the tickets, the one adult told me that he should have known better. I asked him why? He told me that he prosecutes these cases in (a southern county of Minnesota)! I had just given a ticket to an assistant county attorney! They were very understanding and knew I was just doing my job. I thought they would just pay their fine and it would be done with-wrong! They plead not guilty and I was requested to write an offense report for the court. I thought politics were going to get involved. Once they saw my offense report, they plead guilty and each adult paid a fine of $50, plus surcharge of $20, plus court cost of $5. I think they just wanted to see my report and make me earn my pay check!

One deer season, my patrol area contained two different hunting zones. That was always a good spot to work. Some times hunters would be tempted to hunt in the wrong zone for one reason or another. One day while patrolling that line between the two zones, I came upon a deer hunter walking the road. I stopped and checked his license. He had a Zone II license. The south side of the road he was walking on was in Zone II, but it was also a game refuge with no hunting allowed. I asked him which side of the road he was hunting on. He hesitated and finally said the north side which was Zone I. I gave him a ticket for hunting in Zone I with a Zone II license. He paid a fine of $75.

I own some hunting property east of Willow River, Minnesota. Prior to the deer hunting season one year the individual who owns property behind mine called me to tell me that no one had permission to hunt his land that year. I think he suspected that some of his former friends that had hunted there before might try to hunt there again.

Toward the end of the deer season I received a call that my

neighbor had hunters on his property. I went to the property and met the owner and his son. A deputy sheriff was there also. We all observed two hunters come out of my neighbors property pulling a small doe fawn deer that they had shot. I checked their licenses and asked them in the presence of the landowner if he had told them that they couldn't hunt there. They both said that he had told them that they could not hunt his property. I then asked them if they knew who's property their vehicle was parked on. They said, "Curt's" They hesitated and said, "Are you Curt?" I said, "yes, and you don't have permission to be there either!" Both individuals were given tickets for trespassing and the deer was seized. They both paid a $100 fine, surcharge of $10, court cost of $5 and $50 restitution to the landowner. I gave the deer to the landowner. His young son said, "Dad, that's the first deer you ever got."

A farmer caught two individuals shooting a deer from the road on his property. The farmer got the license number of the truck and contacted me. I arrived on the scene, and was trying to figure out what to do next. The license plate came back to a party out of the area. There were lots of deer camps in the area, but I didn't know which one to check. While pondering the situation, along came the suspect truck! Maybe returning to see if they could get another deer. I stopped them. The driver had a particularly full can of beer. I placed it on the hood of the truck. There was no deer in the truck but lots of blood.

Drag mark of a deer poached in Banning State Park.

I asked them where the deer was. They played dumb. They knew nothing about a deer. While looking the truck over and thinking about my next move, one of the individuals accidentally(?) knocked over the beer can. I got mad. I told them I was done playing games. I was going to seize their truck, firearms and everything and charge them with the open bottle unless they told me where the deer was and I meant right now. They told me where the deer was and took me to their camp. I seized the deer and the shooter's 30-06 rifle. I charged him with taking an antlerless deer without a permit. He paid a total of $330 and his rifle was confiscated and sold by the state. I did not charge him with the open bottle.

I can't say enough about the good citizens of Minnesota. One witnessed a deer being shot from Hwy 23 in Banning State Park. The individual got the license number of the vehicle. The most important piece of information in catching a poacher is getting the vehicle license number. I was notified. I went to the location. I observed and took pictures of marks where a deer had been dragged out to the road from the park. I backtracked and found where the deer had been shot and gutted. I made crude drawings of the boot prints left in the snow. The suspect had even left the rubber gloves he had used while gutting the deer. The remains indicated the deer was an adult male. The suspect had a St. Cloud, Minnesota address. I contacted a fellow game warden from that area and told him what I had, including a reliable witness. I asked my fellow officer if he would go and interview the suspect. He did and got an admission. Thanks Dave. I sent the individual a summons for taking a deer in the state park. He paid a fine of $350, plus $250 restituation for the deer.

One night I got a tip that a local hunter had an untagged deer in his shed. I went to his residence. No one answered the door. I thought he might be out in his shed, so I went looking for him. He wasn't there, but the untagged doe was! He also had other tagged deer in the shed. I surmised that he probably was at the local watering hole. I sat in my truck and waited. When he arrived home, I think he was surprised to see me there. I asked him if he had an untagged doe in his shed. He said that he did. I'm glad he didn't try to lie to me. We went and got the deer. I gave him a ticket and seized the deer. He told me that he had accidentally killed the doe while shooting the buck. He was concerned that the deer would not go to waste. I told him that the deer would be going to a lady who did not hunt, and that she liked her deer skinned out right after they had been shot like this one. He offered me a beverage. We shot the bull for awhile and departed still friends.

Untagged deer in a shed.

19

LOADED GUNS

In the fall of the year, one of the most frequent violations conservation officers ran into was the loaded and/or uncased firearm in a motor vehicle. This was a very unsafe practice. In the excitement of spotting game the firearm could go off in the vehicle and kill or injure someone. People thought it was either less work to unload the firearm or that they would have a quicker opportunity at fleeing game. Whatever it was illegal. Usually we could spot a likely violator, by the vehicle slowly moving on a rural, out of the way road. During deer season we could often see the blaze orange clothing they were wearing.

Another thing we watched for was 'furtive' movement. This phrase was coined by my good friend and fellow Game Warden Bob Kangas. Furtive movement was when the driver or passenger spotted us and would try to get their firearms either unloaded or cased up before we got to them. Sometimes it was as little as shoulder movement and sometimes as much as almost turning inside out! It usually didn't work, by the time they saw us it was to late.

One deer season, I was working with another officer and we were following a deputy out to a place where the sheriff's department thought a person of interest to them might also have some illegal venison. We turned down a small township road and spotted two vehicles with a deer hunter in each one. Just before we got to the vehicles the wife jumped out of her vehicle with an uncased firearm. The husband had a loaded firearm and an uncased firearm in his vehicle. I issued both the husband and wife tickets. They were very apologetic and both paid their fines. The next fall I was on some state land across from these good folk's home. I was where I shouldn't have been and got stuck with my squad. I was always getting stuck when I was younger! Guess who showed up with his tractor-the farmer who I'd given the ticket to the year before! He asked if I needed a pull. I said I'd sure appreciate it. He then said that he should charge me the same amount of their fine from last year! I was in a spot so, I said okay. He pulled me out and didn't charge the state a thing! They always were good people and they are still good friends!

One deer season, I observed a pickup moving real slow and stopping every so often on a dead end gravel road. The driver had blaze orange clothing on. There were lots of fields on either side of the road. I guessed he was looking for a deer to shoot. He was so busy looking for deer he didn't even see me right behind him! I timed his stops and jumped out of my squad and ran (I must have been young!) up to the driver's door and opened it. He looked over at me and looked down at his loaded, uncased firearm and started to unload it right in front of me. I said, "Too Late!" He received a ticket and paid a fine of $50.00.

In the years that we had lots of ruffed grouse, lots of people had their firearms loaded and ready to go. One fall in the Nemadji State Forest, my partner and I were checking grouse hunters. We came to an intersection of two forest roads at the same time as a car with a lady riding on the hood with a loaded, uncased shotgun! When their vehicle stopped she slide off and ran to the back door and put the shotgun inside the car! Of course it was to late. I ran and retrieved the firearm and asked the small child in the back seat if they had any birds. The answer was no. Kids are so honest that we didn't have to search the car for over limits. We checked hunting licenses. The lady on the hood didn't have a license! Both ladies got tickets, the driver was a lady too. It cost them a total of $135. They said their husbands weren't going to be to happy with them!

One deer season, my supervisor and good friend Ray Sanbeck and I were checking deer hunters west of Rutledge, Minnesota. We stopped a vehicle driven by an older gentleman with a strong Finish accent. He said a calf had just run across the road. We thought he may be a farmer out rounding up his cattle. We asked him what kind of calf, so we could be on the look out for it. He said a deer calf! Upon further checking we found he had a loaded firearm, he was going to shoot that "calf." He received a ticket instead.

One time, I thought I'd made a mistake and stopped the wrong vehicle. It was midmorning on a Sunday during deer season. The vehicle was moving slowly, so I stopped it. As I approached the vehicle, I could see everyone was dressed in their Sunday go to church clothes. I was already to apologize, until I got to the drivers door and saw that he had a loaded gun in his lap! A little deer hunting on the way home from church! He received a ticket.

Some times deer hunters would make drives. How this worked is hunters would walk though the woods toward other hunters posted on the other side of the woods. In theory, the deer would spook and run toward the posted hunters. If that drive was unsuccessful they would load up and go to another section of woods and repeat the process. One deer season, I was on a road nicknamed Starvation Valley. There was actually a home made sign on the road. I entered Starvation Valley and came over a hill. There before me was every Game Warden's dream. A pickup truck was just pulling onto the road in front of me with nine hunters in the box of the truck and they all had loaded and uncased firearms! Well, I stopped them and asked for licenses and what they were doing. They all had licenses and had just finished a drive and were moving to another location. This could get expensive! I was feeling generous, and not wanting to be officer of the year, I gave them a break. I wrote the driver a ticket for transporting a loaded, uncased firearm and told the rest of the guys that they needed to chip in on the fine. They were all very appreciative! I never caught that bunch doing that again. Sometimes if you can gain compliance of the law you did your job.

One day, during the 1984 deer season, my neighboring officer, Pete Jensen and myself were checking deer hunters. We turned down a small gravel road. We observed a pickup truck heading in our direction. The driver had blaze orange clothing on. We also noticed an uncased firearm on the hood of the vehicle! When the driver finally figured out who we were, it was too late! He did try his best to get out of the violation though. Just before we got to him, he stopped. He jumped out of his truck and very smoothly took the firearm off the hood and walked toward us! We checked his license and I issued him a ticket for transporting a loaded, uncased firearm on a motor vehicle. He paid his $110 fine.

20

TIMBER THEFT

As Minnesota State Conservation Officers we were charged with enforcing all laws pertaining to the Department of Natural Resources (DNR). We were the enforcement branch of the DNR. In this capacity we worked closely with the other DNR divisions. This included forestry, parks, fisheries, wildlife, waters and trails & waterways. When any of these divisions had an enforcement problem they would contact their local conservation officer. I worked closely with all the divisions.

The local forester from Duxbury, Minnesota, had given a firewood permit to an individual to take firewood on a parcel of state land in his district in the fall of 1994. The permit was for birch and maple. When the individual went out to cut his firewood, he noticed a lot of oak trees had been cut down and some had been taken. The logs blocked his way into his firewood permit and he probably wanted to take some of the oak tops for firewood. He immediately reported this to the forester. Two days later, coming to work the forester noticed a truck broke down along the road with a trailer full of red oak logs on it. The forester went out to the site where the firewood permit was issued for. He noticed several oak trees cut into eight foot lengths and where logs had been taken. He also observed tracks and a fresh soft drink can. He returned to the site of the broken down truck and trailer with logs. He observed a partially drank soft drink can on the fender of the trailer. Yes, it was the same brand! The owners of the truck and trailer then returned. Their name was on the side of the truck. He asked them who they were and where they had gotten the logs. They told him their names, but were very evasive as to where they had gotten the logs.

The forester went back to his office and called his supervisors in Moose Lake. They advised him to call me and the sheriff immediately. He then returned to where the truck had been, but it was gone! He met the deputy at that location. The deputy had observed the truck turn off County Road 30 and head north. This information plus a description of the vehicle was relayed to all concerned by radio. A forester from Moose Lake headed south on County 61. He observed a vehicle pull into a location where a person had a small saw mill. It was the suspect vehicle. The forester talked with the vehicle owner and asked where he had gotten the logs. The suspect said he got them off Indian land down by the Lake Lena Reservation. He said they owed him that for taking care of his part-Indian grandchildren. I arrived. The blue pickup that had been at the scene on County Road 30, pulled out and left at a high rate of speed. I stopped the vehicle to question the occupant. It was the suspects son. He was very evasive and the forester thought untruthful! He did state that he and his dad had cut the logs and thought they were on Indian land. They had in fact cut the logs on state and private land without a permit or permission. The foresters went to the site of the stolen logs and cut sections from the stumps and tops. They then went to the saw mill and matched some of the logs with the sections they had taken at the site. The logs were seized.

With this information I went to the suspects house to investigate further. I wanted to tie up all the loose ends, so the right people would be charged and be convicted. The suspect gave me a story. He said that his daughter-in-law was a band member and that he had received permission from a lady at the band office at Lake Lena to take the wood. He also said he had paid for the wood with cash and received no receipt. He denied cutting the logs (remember his son saying they had). He stated that he figured the Indians had cut them. I asked him if he'd seen anyone out there. He said he hadn't seen anyone. I asked him how he knew it was Indians. He said, "You could see where, I'm sure it was Indians running back and forth there." I asked him, "How do you know they were Indians." "Do they leave different tracks or what?" He said, "Well I noticed in one place there was a tailpipe, so I assumed they were in there with a car, and you know, some things like that are earmarks." (I didn't respond to that line of thinking.) He gave me the first name of a lady at Lake Lena that gave them permission to take the wood. I went to find the lady. I wanted to talk to her face to face, but she wasn't around. I called the next day and was able to talk to her. She knew the suspects daughter-in-law, but no permission or permits were given to take any logs off Indian land. I thanked her. I called the Mille Lacs Tribal Government Center. I talked to the individual who gives permits to cut wood on Indian land. He stated that no one had a permit in that area.

I talked to the suspect at length one more time on the phone. I legally tape the conversations. The suspect was very evasive and would not admit guilt, but I did get some damaging information from him. I told him that I couldn't find anyone who had given him or his daughter-in-law permission to take wood any place out there. His response was, "No doubt that's a problem." The suspect said, "I had no idea it wasn't Indian land." I asked the suspect if he thought he was taking the logs off of Indian land illegally. He said, "That was a concern." I tried several more times to talk with his daughter-in-law with no luck. The complaint was filed with the court.

Thanks to all the good work the foresters did, the suspect was found guilty. He was fined $700, surcharge of $140, public defenders cost of $100, court cost of $505, restitution cost of the wood $3092.68 and 90 days in jail that was stayed for one year.

21

DEER SHINERS

People that violate the game and fish laws often try to pattern the game warden's activities. I had an older neighboring officer who fell into a pattern. He always worked deer shiners until 1:30 a.m. His reasoning was the bars closed at 1:00 a.m. After the bars were closed and the potential deer poachers had enough liquid courage in them, that's when their common sense went out the door, and they would decide to go get some venison. If my old neighbor didn't see some shining activity by 1:30 a.m., he'd go home with the mistaken idea that the deer were safe for another night!

When my old neighbor retired, I got a new young officer for a neighbor. He would work me all night sometimes! We didn't always work deer shiners with a crew and the plane. One fall night, I was working with my neighbor. We had a state forester also with us in the back seat. He would often ride along. He would have liked to have become a conservation officer. I was riding in the jump seat. It was my job to get to the driver of the vehicle that we would stop and get him and the vehicle under control. That particular night we had a steady drizzle. The deer didn't seem to mind it and were out. We were poking along on a backcountry road with our lights off looking for any activity. We observed a vehicle approaching on a road that "T" ed on the one we were on. It was 3:00 a.m. The vehicle turned away from us and we decided to follow it without lights to see if the people were up to anything. We came to a field. The suspect vehicle turned into the field and made a swing with it's headlights! Our adrenalin was flowing, we had probable cause to stop the vehicle to see if they had any firearms capable of taking a big game animal! We waited until the vehicle was leaving on the field approach road. My partner made an excellent stop! He hit his lights and red lights as he blocked the vehicle's exit. I was out of the squad with my flashlight and at the vehicles drivers door in an instant. I jerked the door open. The interior light came on. I observed the passenger holding a 20 gauge shotgun slug. I knew it was 20 gauge because it was yellow. I could see the lead end of the slug. Both the driver and passenger were looking at me with their mouths open! I reached in and turned off and removed the ignition key. All the while, I was hollering to my partner, "He's got a 20 gauge slug!" This all took place in a matter of seconds. My partner was at the passenger door right now! The passenger still had time to drop the slug under the seat. My partner found that slug and another the passenger had in his pocket. Now where is the gun? The vehicle was a hatchback. In the back seat we could see the barrel of a firearm sticking out alongside the hatchback. It was a 20 gauge shotgun! They said they weren't looking to shoot deer, they were looking for skunks to shoot. The law says it is against the law to shine any wild animal while in possession of an implement capable of taking a big game animal. They had just admitted to gross misdemeanor shining! We arrested both individuals, seized the vehicle, gun and shells. John got a search warrant and we inventoried the vehicle the next day. John figured out how they would get the gun when they were ready to shoot a deer. When they reached back from the front seat and grabbed the barrel of their firearm the hatchback folded down and the firearm could be pulled from what you would call the trunk area. Not a bad try on trying to circumvent the law! Both individuals were found guilty and paid a large fine. The poachers were no longer safe in that area after 1:30 a.m.!

My first involvement in a shining arrest happened while I was on training. For the first three to six months after we were hired as conservation officers we would travel around the state and work with field officers who would train us in the right way (and sometimes wrong ways!) to do your job.

I was working with a training officer the first fall on the job. We were set up on a field where he had some complaints of deer shining. We sat on the hood of his squad with sleeping bags to keep off the fall chill. He liked to sit outside in case we heard a shot in the distance. He knew his area well enough to have a pretty good idea of where to go if he heard shots in any particular direction. If you sat in the warm vehicle, even with the window down, you would not get an accurate location of a shot heard. Often, chasing shots didn't produce an arrest. We chased one shot that night, but no vehicles were found. Along about quitting time (anytime when a warden got tired), he said lets head for the barn. Driving with our lights on, we came over a hill and there in front of us was a vehicle pulled into a hayfield approach with it's headlights shining onto the field! We were no longer tired! My training officer pulled right up to the drivers door. We jumped out and the driver got out also. My partner took the driver back to the squad and told me to go get the gun! I hadn't seen a gun? I went and opened the door of the suspects vehicle and shined my flashlight in the car. There was the uncased, loaded high power! Later, my training officer had to laugh, he knew I had found the gun because he heard me say in a loud voice, "Holy cow!" The individual was arrested and I got to drive the suspects vehicle to jail. The firearm and vehicle were seized. The individual paid a large fine.

I was working with a shining crew mid-October 1981. My Partner, John was in the jump seat. We had the "eye in the sky." The eye in the sky called me and told me to fire up and head west as soon as I could. He had observed a vehicle shining fields in that direction. After going west for a short time, the pilot told me to turn north, which I did. Again the pilot told me that the suspect vehicle was heading in our direction and that I should turn off my lights and find a spot to pull off and wait. I backed into a small gravel road off the main road. I informed the pilot that we could see a vehicle heading south turn toward us on the gravel road. The pilot said that was the vehicle shining and that we should stop it. At just the right time, (when the suspect vehicle was left with no options except to stop) I turned on my lights and red lights. The vehicle stopped and my partner jumped out and secured the vehicle. The two individuals had a 30-30 rifle, a strung bow with arrows, hunting knives, ammo, a flashlight, a garbage bag (for meat?) a bow and arrow license and a copy of the 1981 hunting regulations. We radioed the State Patrol dispatcher with the individuals drivers license numbers so we knew who we were dealing with. The dispatcher called back and asked by code (10-12) if we had the suspects where they could hear. I told the dispatcher they were not able to hear the transmission. The dispatcher informed me that one of the individuals was absent without leave from the marine corp.! We hand cuffed both suspects. The local officer who was also working with the crew arrived and we turned everything over to him. The individuals went to jail and their vehicle and equipment were seized.

The case went to trial in Kanebec County. I was on the witness stand being questioned by the defense attorney. He was trying to get me to admit to an illegal search. His question to me was, "Officer, how did you see the strung bow." I paused for a second, then answered, "With my eyes." The judge dropped his head on the bench and started laughing! The defense attorney, was saying, "No, no that's not what I mean!" We won the case. The marines, two very tough looking guys with short hair and dressed in suits, were waiting for their AWOL man! They were not gentle with their man! They slammed him up against the wall and handcuffed him and almost carried him out the door! I think he was in trouble!

My neighboring officer, Pete Jensen, and I were set up near Grindstone Lake in a complaint area looking for deer poachers. Well after dark, we observed two vehicles traveling slowly close together on the paved county road. The first vehicle was shinning a spotlight out the passenger's window! We followed behind the second vehicle without lights. The second vehicle had plenty of opportunity to pass the first vehicle, but didn't. We guessed that the second vehicle contained the shooter. Often poachers would do this to try to avoid an arrest. If we would stop the vehicle shining, they would have no firearm. No firearm meant no arrest in those days. The question was, how are we going to stop both vehicles at once? I told Pete that I was going to blow by the second vehicle and stop the first, essentially blocking the road for the second vehicle. It was Pete's job to get to the second vehicle and I would get to the first one. I sped up and blew by the trailing vehicle with no lights on. I then turned on my red lights and siren and pulled slightly in front of the first vehicle. They stopped. Pete was out in a flash and at the second car. I jumped out and secured the first car. I immediately recognized the couple. The husband was driving and the wife was working the spotlight. The second car contained another couple known to both Pete and I. They were friends of the first couple. We found no firearms in either vehicle. This was before the misdemeanor shinning law, so no arrests were made. They did say that we scared the heck out of them, especially the trailing car when we blew by them with no lights! I don't think it was their first time, because the wife had already stuck the spotlight under the seat before I got to their car.

22

FISHING II

One summer, I received a call from a lady. She stated that she had been sitting on her dock dangling her bare feet in the water, when a muskie bit her on the foot! I asked her how big the muskie was. She told me it was 37 inches long. I suspected something when she told me such an exact number. I asked her how she knew it was that long. She told me that they had a rod and reel ready to go on the dock and they cast out and caught the fish. I asked her what they did with the fish. She said, "We killed it." I told her good. Even though it was not of legal size to keep, I didn't think we needed people-eating musky in the lake. A couple of years after I retired, I heard that another musky in the same area had bitten a child wading in the water. I hope the man-eating trait isn't in the musky genes in that lake!

One summer day, Bob Kangas and myself were checking fishing activity on one of my lakes. We checked a boat with no current registration on it. There were two guys in the boat. Only one of the individuals was fishing. I asked the boat operator for his fishing license. It was current. I asked him for a drivers license. I planned on writing him a ticket for not displaying current registration on a watercraft. The information I needed for the ticket is much easier to get from the drivers license. He handed me his drivers license. The drivers license was from North Dakota, but the fishing license he had shown me was a Minnesota resident license! They had a problem. After interviewing the suspects, we found out the fishing license belonged to the individual who wasn't fishing! The individual that was fishing was from North Dakota and did not have a Minnesota non-resident fishing license. The other person in the boat was a Minnesota resident. He had lent his fishing license to his North Dakota buddy. The non-resident fisherman was given a ticket for fishing without a non-resident license. His fine for that was $50. (1980) He was also given a ticket for failure to display the registration on the boat. He paid a $15 fine for that. His Minnesota friend, who had borrowed him the license, was given a ticket for lending a license. His fine was $100. The best part was when the Minnesota resident admitted to us that he had just been admitted to law school!

Occasionally, someone had left their fishing license at home. In that case, I had two options: I could ticket them for not having their license in possession or I could have them sign an affidavit that they had purchased a license. If the individual signed an affidavit, they would have to send me their license along with a self-addressed stamped envelope. After I looked at the license, I would send it back to them. I usually gave the person the second option.

One summer day, I checked a lady fishing on Big Pine Lake. She did not have a fishing license with her. She assured me that she did have one, but had left it at home in the twin cities. I had her sign an affidavit as to when and where she had bought the license. I told her to send it to me, with the self-addressed stamped envelope, within seven days or I would be sending her a ticket. She agreed. The license never came. I mailed her two tickets. One ticket for no fishing license and one for making a false affidavit. The lady failed to show up on her court date. That was not a good idea! The judge issued a bench warrant for her arrest. That got her attention. She paid a fine of $85 for the no license charge and a fine of $145 for making the false affidavit. It would have been much easier and cheaper to have just admitted to me that she didn't have a license in the first place.

I had a number of small lakes in my patrol area. These lakes often didn't have public accesses. I think fishermen thought that they wouldn't be checked on these small lakes. I guessed that they figured that I would be spending all my time on the bigger lakes that had public accesses. Wrong! I did check the smaller lakes too. I often found people violating the fish and game laws on these smaller lakes.

One late May, I checked a fisherman on one of these small lakes. The fisherman did have a fishing license. He also had six bass, two sunfish and two crappie. The only thing wrong was that it wasn't bass season yet! I gave him a ticket for taking bass in closed season. I seized all his fish and he paid a $75 fine.

I caught lots of fishermen fishing with extra lines. These fishermen, with extra lines, where usually fishing through the ice, from anchored boats or from shore.

One day, while checking fishing activity on Oak Lake, I found a lone fisherman trolling with two lines. Trolling is when the boat is being propelled by a motor and you are dragging a lure behind the boat through the water. The fisherman had a cane pole out one side of the boat and a rod and reel out the other side. He got a ticket for fishing with two lines. I wondered what he would have done if he would have gotten bites on both lines at the same time. I thought I would never see someone trolling with two lines again, but I did! On Big Pine Lake I caught a guy trolling with two rods and reels. He was using a flatfish for bait on each outfit. He also got a ticket for fishing with two lines. I never encountered this situation again in my career.

One spring in 1977, just before the northern pike/walleye opener, I was working with my neighboring conservation officer. We decided to see what if anything was going on along the Kettle River near Sandstone, Minnesota. We found a vehicle parked near the dam. Yes, there used to be a dam on the Kettle River in Sandstone! We walked along the river below the dam and observed two individuals fishing. We snuck up on them and asked to see their fishing licenses. One individual had a license and one didn't have one. They also had six northern pike on a stringer! I wrote each a ticket for taking northern pike in closed season. They both paid a fine of $45. The individual without a fishing license got a ticket for that too. His fine was $35 for no fishing license. We also confiscated all six northern pike.

23

DAD'S GUN

One late fall, I received a call from a local resident. He advised me that he had just caught his neighbor and his neighbor's wife shooting a deer on his field. It was late at night, so I took the information and told him I'd take care of it in the morning.

I knew the suspected violator. I went out to his home the next morning. I parked behind his pickup truck. Walking up to the house, I couldn't help but notice what appeared to be blood in the box of the truck! The suspected violator answered the door. I think he knew that I was coming, because he was acting very nervous. I asked him where the deer was that he had shot the night before. He told me to come in, that it was in the freezer. He opened the freezer and showed me the deer. He had gutted and skinned it out. I told him to get me the gun that he had shot the deer with. He brought me the firearm. I took the firearm and the deer out to my squad. I took pictures and samples of the blood on his truck. I then issued him a ticket for deer shinning. I didn't feel it was necessary to ticket his wife too.

Before I left, the violator had one request. He wanted to know how he could get the gun back-it was his dad's. I told him that if he came to court, plead guilty and paid his fine, I would give him his dad's gun back.

He plead guilty and paid a fine of $1,100. I gave him back the firearm.

Another good case made, thanks to the excellent cooperation I had from the people in my area.

Dad's gun with poached deer.

24

A DANGEROUS BUSINESS

Bob Kangas was my neighboring officer. We made a lot of great cases working together. I wish I would have been there with him on this case.

This is Bob's story in his own words.

Working deer shiners was a way of life for Minnesota game wardens from the 4th of July through December. All the people we encountered shining at night had firearms in various forms of being uncased and/or loaded in their vehicles. Wardens usually had the element of surprise on their side when they stopped a car shining an artificial light on a field. The shiners were hoping to find a deer to shoot. Most vehicles we stopped doing this activity did not try to run, because we usually blocked their vehicle and were out of our squads and at their vehicle before the perpetrators figured out what was happening. At the most, they would be hurrying to try to unload or case up their firearms. It was always too late for them.

We had a work party scheduled on the night of October 23, 1981, along the Pine County and Kanabec County line. Work crews at night involving aircraft had two officers per squad car. The warden plane would fly over the area for most of the night trying to spot suspicious vehicles shining lights, looking for deer. Game warden squads would be strategically located throughout the area in hiding places. All wardens had a map of the area to be worked, and they knew the other squads locations, and areas that had been shining problems. The pilot would direct the closest squad to the area where a vehicles had been spotted shining a light. Those violators didn't have a chance. The aircraft would keep them in sight until a squad had them stopped.

I, Bob Kangas, was stationed in Hinckley, Minnesota, at that time. My position that night was at a spot west of Friesland, Minnesota. It was a very dark night because of the cloud cover. When I was nearing my hiding spot, about three miles west of Friesland, the dispatcher notified all the squads that the pilot, out of Brainerd, Minnesota, had cancelled his flight because of low clouds. I heard most of the wardens, including my rider from Pine City, Minnesota, call to say that they were not coming. I heard one officer say that he was on his spot about fifteen miles away from me and was going to stay and work for awhile. Since I was almost to my hiding spot, I decided to pull in and watch the field across the road from my spot. I had been driving with my sneak light for the last couple of miles to my hiding spot, because I didn't want to scare off any potential violators with my headlights. What we called a sneak light was actually a military blackout light mounted on the front of our squads.

I pulled my squad, a pickup truck, into an abandoned farm on the north side of the county road. It was positioned so I could see over some low bushes onto a field to my south across the county road. This was a field of about thirty acres that I could see. The field always had deer feeding on it at night. Just as I finished pouring a cup of coffee out of my thermos bottle, about ten minutes after I arrived, I noticed a small light at the far end of the field. I hadn't seen or heard a vehicle drive onto the field, even though I was standing outside my squad.

My next thought was that there was a foot shiner out on the field. These folks, as the name implies, don't use a vehicle to poach, but they would walk the fields with a gun and a light to try to shoot a deer. They usually are local people who know the area and usually walk from home or get dropped off from a vehicle driven by their partner in crime. They also, always ran when confronted by a game warden.

Putting my coffee down, I grabbed my flashlight and binoculars and walked closer to the road, so I could see better. The light that I was seeing would be on for a few seconds and then it would be off. I could see some movement through my binoculars when the light was on, but, I could not tell how many people were out there. I wondered how I was going to catch these guys, if there were more than one, by myself. As I said, foot shiners always run. I would always go for the one with the firearm, because having the gun in court was excellent evidence of intent to take deer.

The old saying that patience is a virtue is so true and should be a trait of all good game wardens. I learned this from an old timer who I trained with. So, instead of moving toward the light on the field, I waited. The light started coming toward me! As it got closer, I could see through my binoculars that there were two individuals.

I positioned myself behind some bushes for concealment, but I could still see the field. After a few minutes of waiting and watching, I could make out that one of the individuals was using a flashlight and the other one was carrying a long gun, either a rifle or a shotgun. They were walking right toward me and soon came to the county road directly across from where I was hidden.

The two were about fifty feet from me when they stopped at the road with their light off. I then noticed the glow of headlights to the west of us. They saw them too, and started running across the road and up the approach right toward me. One of them said, "let's get that #&#& deer." I quickly realized that they had a deer down. They were going to get it when they were spooked by the headlights.

Since I am right handed, I always carried my flashlight in my left hand, leaving my gun hand free. I turned my flashlight on and pointed it at the poachers when they were about twenty feet from me. I said, "Freeze, State Game Warden!" Those words stopped them in their tracks. In an instant, things turned bad. The guy with the flashlight turned it on and pointed it at me. The other guy quickly put his gun to his shoulder and fired one shot, hitting me dead center in the chest. The force of the bullet hitting me in my bullet proof vest knocked me backwards and to the ground. As I was turning around to the prone position, My thought was that he was going to shoot me again.

I unholstered my .38 service revolver as I hit the ground. I was expecting to be in a gun fight. The two turned and ran back down the approach where they had come from. I was sure that they were going to turn around and shoot at me some more. I fired four rounds at them, missing on all four. I had my flashlight shining on them as they hit the county road. They ran toward the west. All this transpired in only a few seconds.

As I got up and ran after them, the car with the headlights that had spooked them showed up. It stopped. The driver said that he could smell gunpowder and he was wondering what was going on. After I explained to him what had happened , he told me that he had seen the two individuals running down the road. He thought that they had went to a farmhouse a quarter of a mile to the west of us. With this information, I had went back to my squad and called the dispatcher on the radio with a "10-88," which means that an officer needs help.

The first officer to arrive was a state trooper. He met me on the county road at the driveway that went to the house where I suspected the two felons to be. At about that time another officer, a deputy, arrived, three people came walking down the driveway toward us. Two of them looked like the guys who had shot me. The other was a women who claimed to be the mother of one of the boys. She told us the boys had ran into the house and said that they were scared, because they had just shot "Bigfoot." We immediately took the boys into custody and told the mother what had happened. She didn't understand what all the fuss was about, since no one had gotten hurt! It turned out that both boys were only fifteen years old.

We went back to the crime scene after the deputy took the boys to jail. I found the gun they used to shoot me. It was a .22 caliber single shot rifle. The shooter had thrown it to the side of the approach when they started to run away. After securing the scene and gathering the evidence I needed, I drove to the hospital to get checked out. All x-rays showed that no serious damage had been done to me by the impact of the bullet to my bullet proof vest. Although, I would have a major bruise the size of a baseball for several weeks in the middle of my chest.

The empty shell casing was still in the rifle. It was a .22 long rifle. The vest I was wearing was not rated to stop a narrow diameter bullet, with high velocity, fired from such a short distance of twenty feet. The crime lab said that the bullet had penetrated all the layers of the Kevlar in the vest except the last one, thankfully!

These two boys were found guilty of assault and sentenced to juvenile correction centers until they turned eighteen. They tried to claim the gun went off accidentally, but an expert from the state crime lab testified that could not have happened. I heard that they were constantly in trouble at the detention centers. They tried to escape, damaged property (including police cars), etc. As the years went on, one of the boys took his own life and I understand the other one did also.

The Minnesota Conservation Officers Association included bullet proof vests in their bargaining with the State of Minnesota for safety equipment just a year or two before I got shot wearing mine. This was a life saver for me as well as for at least one other Minnesota officer I know who was involved in a vehicle crash.

Being a game warden was a lifestyle, not just a job. The career brings you outdoors in all climates, is rigorous, fulfilling and too short for thirty years. It can also be a dangerous business. I wouldn't have had it any other way.

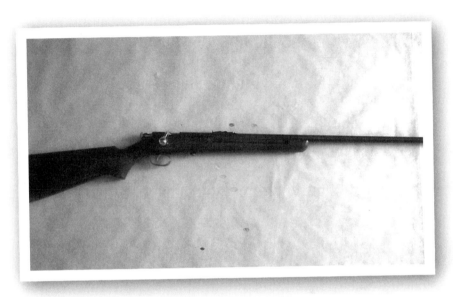

Firearm Bob was shot with.

25

THE GOOD CUSTOMER

An individual from southern Minnesota purchased a piece of property in my patrol area. He intended to use the property for rifle deer hunting. The property was 20 acres in size. The shape of the property was a problem. It was a half a mile long and only 110 yards wide. Even if he sat in the middle of his property, he would only be 55 yards from both his north and south line. This caused trespass problems. The individual would usually bring four or five friends to hunt deer on his property. With so little property to hunt, the individual would be road hunting on the morning of opening day. I got to know him quite well!

The first time I met him, he had a loaded firearm in his vehicle. He got a ticket that cost him $100.

The following year, he was driving his tractor on a minimum maintenance road near his property. He had no blaze orange clothing on and, yes, he also had a loaded, uncased deer rifle with him! Another $100 ticket, plus a written warning for no blaze orange.

A few years later, on opening day of deer season, I came driving over a hill in the road and there he was again. This time he was standing in the middle of the road by his truck. He was pointing his rifle unto a local farmer's field. I asked him, by name, just what he was doing. He told me that he had seen a deer on the field and was going to shoot it. I told him that he couldn't shoot from the roadway and if he shot unto the field, he would be trespassing. He told me that he had permission from the farmer. I told him that I knew the farmer and that he wasn't giving anyone permission to hunt that year. I kind of yelled at him and told him to quit road hunting. He wasn't given a ticket because he hadn't shot and it wasn't illegal to be standing on the road with a loaded firearm. This time he did get a ticket for no blaze orange.

A few years later, just after dark on a rainy night in deer season, I came upon a vehicle on the side of the road. The vehicle was running with it's lights on. I stopped to see if they were having some problem. The driver, dressed in blaze orange, told me that he was waiting for his hunting partner to come out of the woods. I checked the drivers firearm. It was loaded. I gave him a $100 ticket. When his partner came out of the woods, I identified him as my good old customer! He had a license, but I guessed that he was trespassing. I asked him if he had permission to be on the posted property. He told me that he had gotten permission from the landowner. The landowner lived just up the road. I told the individual that I was going to check with the landowner and if he didn't have permission, I would be coming over to his camp and giving him a ticket for trespassing. He still maintained that he had permission. After I left the hunters, I went to the landowner's house. The landowner stated that the individual did NOT have permission. I went to the violator's camp. I gave him a ticket for trespassing in front of his hunting buddies. I wish I could have given him a ticket for lying to me. I had a good talk with all of them about trespassing and transporting loaded firearms.

I checked the individual once more in my career. He must have gotten tired of paying fines, because his firearm was unloaded and properly cased, but he was still on the road looking for deer!

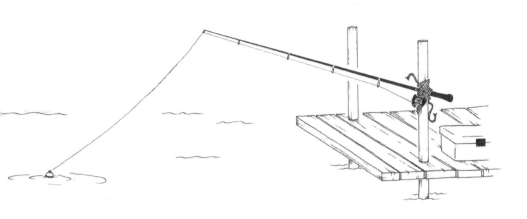

26

UNATTENDED
FISHING LINES

It is against the law to leave a fishing line unattended. Most of the time I would find unattended lines off a dock or in an unoccupied fish house. People would bait their lines and then leave to do something else. When they came back at a later time, they hoped to find a fish on their line.

One summer day, I was patrolling one of the lakes in my patrol area. I usually slowly trolled around the lakes looking for unattended lines and observing fishermen on the lake. I spotted a couple of bobbers connected to lines from a dock. No one was on or near the dock. I pulled up to the dock. I tied my boat up to the dock and got out and reeled up the unattended lines. I took the lines up to the cabin and knocked on the door. There was no answer. Looking around, it looked like no one had been at the cabin for some time. The shades were pulled and there was no sign that a vehicle had been in the driveway.

I had noticed people sitting down by their dock at the next cabin. They had been watching my every move. I walked over and asked them if they knew who's lines were left off the dock. They knew nothing. I had a good idea that they had put their lines off the neighbor's dock. I was unable to get a confession. I seized the fishing equipment and left a seizure receipt at the unoccupied cabin. I never heard from anyone. I turned the equipment into the state for sale on the auction.

I had learned a valuable lesson. When ever I saw an unattended lines after that, I observed them for a while before showing my hand.

I was patrolling a lake with my neighboring officer in his area one evening. We came upon a line and a bobber off a dock. No one was in sight. We felt we had a violation of an unattended line. We tied up to the dock, but could not find a rod and reel. We grabbed the line and followed it up the dock and across the lawn. The line went up to and into the closed door of the cabin! We knocked and an individual answered the door. He had the rod and reel inside the cabin with him. What a lot of work to avoid a ticket and still not have to sit on the dock and watch his bobber!

Five years after I retired, I was at an American Legion meeting. After the meeting I was talking to a few of my fellow legionnaires. I found out one of them lived on a local lake. I kiddingly told him that I couldn't remember ever giving him a ticket. He told us he had been given a ticket for an unattended line in the early 1980's. His story was that he was putting some posts in his yard when a conservation officer tapped him on the shoulder. The officer asked him if the rod and reel that had been off the dock was his. He told the officer it was and was given a ticket. He told us that I wasn't the officer. He said, "It was a nice, young officer." Another legionnaire said, "That was Curt!" I went home and looked him up in my ticket files. It was me who had given him the $27.50 ticket in 1981. I guess, I was a nice, young officer back then!

The sneakiest violator of the unattended line law was the individual who had his rod and reel onshore with his line out and no bobber. I spotted the rod and reel and thought it was odd that it was lying near the water pointing toward the lake. Upon investigating, I found the baited line out. I located the individual and gave him a ticket.

Another day, I spotted two unattended lines off a dock. No one was around. Some one was some place though, because there was a car in the yard and the cabin was open. I grabbed the lines and went looking for the violators. I finally found them. They were out fishing! Both gentlemen from South Dakota received tickets and posted bail with me. I suppose I could have also given them tickets for fishing with two lines, but that might have been a little chicken.

I seized an unattended line off a dock one day. No one was around, but it looked like someone was up for the weekend. I came back later that day and found a couple of guys at the cabin. They had been out golfing! I gave the individual who owned the unattended line a ticket. He wasn't very happy with me. He thought that he should be given a break because of all the taxes they paid.

Mille Lacs Lake had tons of winter fishermen. The resorts on the lake would plow main roads on the ice out to their customer's fish houses. I would often go and assist my fellow officers stationed on the lake. One Saturday night, I was there assisting my neighboring officer. It was just after the supper hour, when I noticed lots of vehicles heading back out on the lake from the resort. I was guessing that they had been at the resort for supper. I told my partner to follow one back to their fish house. We did and sure enough they had left lines down unattended while they had gone to the resort for supper. We did the same thing five more times that night and found unattended lines each time.

27

WINTER FISHING

One of the hardest arrest to make in the winter or summer was what we called double tripping. Double tripping is when an individual would catch a limit of fish, take them home, and then return to try to catch more in the same day. Some people thought that if they gave the first limit away they could take another. Wrong, the law only allowed one limit per day no matter what you did with the fish.

One winter I received information that a certain individual was taking a lot of fish. I was told that he would take a limit, go home and come back for more. The poacher lived on one of the lakes in my area. I went to work on him. I observed his fish house from a distance through my binoculars. I could tell he was at his fish house because I could see his vehicle parked next to it. Late morning, he left his fish house with a bag of something. I guessed it was fish. After the lunch hour, I observed him return to his fish house. I waited until I figured he had time to catch more fish. I went to his fish house to check him. The fisherman had one northern pike. I asked him how many he had caught that morning. He told me that he had caught three that morning and had given them to his wife at home. I told him that was not legal and that he had taken one northern over the limit for the day. I gave him a ticket and seized the extra northern. I did let him keep the three fish he had caught that morning. He also did not have his name and address on his fish house. He got a ticket for that too. He paid $49 for the extra northern and $27 for the no name or address violation. I think the fines have increased since this mid 1980's arrest.

Once in awhile, I'd find a lady violating the law. Checking fishermen on Oak Lake one winter day, I found a lady in a fish house with five lines down! She got a ticket for three extra lines and paid a fine of $145 in 1999.

Fishing with two lines in the winter is legal. The law doesn't say that you have to fish with two lines though! I checked a winter fisherman whose auger quite after drilling one hole. He just had to take advantage of the legal ability to use two lines, so he had two lines down the same 8 inch hole! Oh, by the way he didn't have a fishing license. The ticket cost him $44 in 1985.

I was working with a crew of game wardens on Mille Lacs Lake one winter night. We would check a group of fish houses all at once. The house I checked in one group had an individual in it with multiple lines down. The guy was going to get a ticket. Before I could issue the ticket, the officer whose area it was arrived at the same house. Since it was his area, I figured I'd let him make the call and write the ticket. I told the young officer what I had and asked him what he wanted to do. The young officer looked at the violator and recognized him. Dave said, "We're taking everything." And we did! We even took the rattle reels off the wall. This was the third time Dave had ran into this violator fishing with too many lines. He got a ticket and lost his equipment. We sent him a message that violators would not be tolerated.

Fish houses had to be removed from the lake at a certain time each year. The weather sometimes made this difficult. People would take the owner information off the houses and either burn them or just leave them for us to take off. Game wardens could usually tell which houses would be left. The good expensive ones we didn't worry about. It was the cheap shacks that we marked for later identification. Some fisherman would pull their houses off the lake and leave them on the public access blocking use of the access. One individual got tickets from me for that two years in a row before he wised up!

28

DEER POACHER

One mid October, I received a call from a dear friend that he had heard a shot at sundown. He suspected his neighbor had poached a deer. I contacted my neighboring officer to see if he was available to help me catch this poacher.

We arrived at the poachers farm just after dark. We observed a light on in the barn. We went to the barn and knocked on the door.

The poacher said, "Come on in." I don't know who he was expecting, but he sure had a surprised look on his face when he saw us! He was in the process of skinning the poached buck fawn. There were two firearms leaning against the wall. I asked the individual which firearm he had shot the deer with. He said, "Both." He had shot the deer with the 12 gauge single shot with buckshot and then finished it off with the .22. The poacher showed me where he had first shot the deer from. I found the spent buckshot casing on the ground. I seized both firearms and the deer.

The individual was given a ticket for taking a deer in closed season. He paid a fine of $300 and lost both firearms. I placed the empty shell casing in the shotgun and turned both firearms into the state through my supervisor after the case was settled. They went to the auction to be sold. The lady who checked all the firearms going on the sale was startled when she opened the shotgun and out popped a shell! No one else had bothered to check it up the whole chain of command.

The remains of several poached deer.

Poached deer hanging in the woods.

29

ATV'S SNOWMOBILES

Through my work station in northern Pine County runs a paved recreation trail. The Willard Munger Trail was made on the old railroad bed after the tracks and ties were taken up. The Minnesota Department of Natural Resources (DNR) owns and maintains the trail. Uses allowed are: In the winter, while snow covered, snowmobiles may operate on the trail with proper permits and registration. Also, snowmobilers must obey the traffic signs and a speed limit of no more the 50 miles per hour. Summer (no snow cover times) use is restricted to hikers and bikers. Bikers must also obey the traffic signs. No all terrain vehicles (ATV's) allowed!

I often got complaints of ATV's illegally on the trail. One reoccurring complaint was of an ATV ripping up and down the trail after dark right in the town of Willow River. I needed to try to put a stop to this illegal activity. One night I hide my squad and walked to the trail and hide behind a utility pole next to the trail. Sure enough, after a short wait here comes the ATV! I jumped out from behind my hiding spot. The driver of the ATV could plainly see me, but wasn't going to stop! I did an overhand shine of my flashlight to try to identify the ATV or driver. To my horror, my heavy-duty aircraft aluminum flashlight slipped out of my hand! It went end over end and smacked the driver on the shoulder! That will leave a bruise! The driver didn't stop. I retrieved my flashlight (no damage) and went home. I never did find out who the individual was, but I had no more complaints in that location.

In late February, I was in my squad on County Road 61 heading to Rutledge from Willow River. County Road 61 runs right along side the Munger trail at this location. I observed a pair of snowmobiles heading south on the trail. I pulled along side of them and determined that they were not speeding. I did notice that the one machine did not appear to have current registration displayed on it. I pulled ahead of the snowmobiles and stopped at a crossing about a mile ahead of them. I wanted to stop them there to check their registration. I was out of sight of them. After a short time, they hadn't showed up! Something was wrong. Maybe they pulled off somewhere or had stopped on the trail. I headed back north to see if I could find them. There they were headed north on the trail! They had turned around for some reason. I again passed them and stopped at the next crossing to wait for them. Again, after a short time, they didn't show up! I headed south again. There they were headed south also. I figured out they were avoiding me! I hung back so they didn't know I was once again behind them. I followed them until they reached a spot where a trail left the main trail and crossed County Road 61. They had to stop for the county road. I sped up and blocked the crossing just ahead of them. It was a father and son. The father told me that he hadn't had time to register his machine and his young sons machine had never been registered. He admitted that they were trying to avoid me. I issued the father two tickets. One for operating an unregistered snowmobile and one for allowing the operation of an unregistered snowmobile. Fines, surcharge and court cost: $170.00

Willow River holds an annual fishing contest. When I first got to Willow River it was held at Long Lake near Rutledge, Minnesota. Recently, it has always been held at the dam on the north edge of Willow River. I always attend, mostly for public relations purposes. I never checked licenses, because there were always kids and people running all over! I t was fun just talking to people.

One year, I noticed an individual was sitting on a snowmobile with no current registration on it. I asked him if his machine was registered. He said it wasn't. I told him I wouldn't give him a ticket at the contest, but he must go directly home after the contest and not ride his machine until he got it registered. He agreed.

After the contest, I met up with my neighboring warden to work snowmobilers. We set up on a trail on our snowmobiles and stopped and checked machines as they came by. Guess who came driving by? The same guy that I had warned at the fishing contest! He was heading in the opposite direction from his home. I never said a word, I just got out my ticket book and wrote him up. He paid his fine of $44.00.

Dangerous encounters on snowmobile trails not only involve other machines or automobiles, but sometimes wildlife.

One winter, an individual drove his damaged snowmobile into Willow River and I was contacted. The individual had hit three deer with his machine! He was able to limp back to town with his damaged snowmobile. The accident took place near the rock cuts by Denham, Minnesota. After making sure the individual was alright, other then slightly nerve racked, I went out to the area of the accident. I found two dead deer and evidence where another deer had limped off with a none fatal injury. I salvaged both deer. That snowmobiler was lucky he wasn't seriously injured.

The next incident involved myself! I was heading west on the trail west of Denham on my snowmobile. It was daylight and I was traveling at a speed somewhat under the 50 mile per hour limit. There was a thicket of small spruce trees right along the trail. Unbeknownst to me the landowner was feeding deer right on the other side of this thicket! Out jumped a deer right unto the hood of my machine! My windshield was bent back and knocked the red light from my machine. The deer continued on its merry way. I was a little shook, but it appeared my machine sustained no damage. My red light laid on the trail behind me in pieces. I went back and picked up the pieces and found out they just snapped back together. I was relieved it hadn't broken. (no explaining to my supervisor!) For some reason my machine just wasn't running right. I stopped my snowmobile and opened the hood to see if I could figure out what was wrong. My spark plug was broken. The hood had flexed enough, without breaking, from being hit by the deer that it broke the spark plug! I replaced the plug and was off again, but I was really looking around for deer!

30

BEAR HUNTERS

One fall, I received a tip that bear hunters north of the county line had unsigned bear baits. Bear baits had to be registered and a sign had to be placed within ten feet of the bait and no more then six feet above the ground. Also the sign had to be a certain size. This was so conservation officers would know whose baits were whose in case of any illegal activity. The bait pile also could not contain any cans, plastics or glass.

The county line was my area border. My neighboring officer was gone at that time, so I planned on checking out the complaint. The borders between two officers tended to get worked less then other areas in their patrol districts. I don't know for sure, but officers might have assumed that the other guy was working the border. Also, the borders tended to be farther from their homes. I often wondered if violators considered this when they poached? The county line was also the line between the no-quota and quota zones for bear hunting. The no-quota license was unlimited and could be purchased over the counter. The quota license had to be applied for and there were a limited number of these.

Baiting was allowed a week before the season. I walked into the baits just before season. I found the two baits and neither one was registered or signed. Both baits also contained illegal material. Bear hunters usually only hunt in the late afternoon or evening hours. I planned to be back and catch the hunters on stand on opening evening. I contacted my southern neighboring officer, Pete Jensen, to assist me in catching these violators.

We walked into the stands late afternoon of opening day. The first stand had a bow hunter in it. Checking his license, I found that he had a no-quota license in the quota zone. We seized his bow and arrows and I issued him a ticket for having the wrong license and one for hunting over an unregistered/unsigned bait. I also issued him a written warning for illegal material in his bait.

The second bait was several hundred yards from the first one. While in route to the second stand we heard a shot. When we got to the second stand we found another hunter with a no-quota license. He had just shot a bear with his muzzle loader! This hunter also received two tickets and a written warning for the same offenses. We seized his weapon too. We got them to volunteer to drag out the bear for us. The bear was seized and confiscated. I sold the bear to a local church that was having a wild game feed. After both hunters paid their large fines, I returned their weapons to them.

The individual who gave me the information received a TIP reward.

Photography by Christine

ABOUT THE AUTHOR

Curt Rossow was born in Faribault, Minnesota. He grew up in rural Owatonna, Minnesota. He graduated from the University of Minnesota with a degree in forestry/wildlife. He was drafted into the US Army upon graduation. He spent one year in Vietnam. Upon returning to the real world, he married Martha Anderson on March 4, 1972. He was hired as a Conservation Officer (Game Warden) by the State of Minnesota on June 13, 1973. His first station was Austin, Minnesota. After that two plus year assignment, he transferred to the Willow River, Minnesota station. He spent the next twenty-six years working as a field officer in the Willow River area, retiring on August 14, 2001.

Curt and Martha raised four children: Heidi, Benjamin, Rachel, and Daniel. They now have seven grandchildren.

Curt continues serving the people of Pine County as County Commissioner.